Astrid Berger • Gabriele Broniowski

Aufsteigen ... in ENGLISCH 4

So schaffst du die 4. Klasse HS/AHS und Neue Mittelschule

G&G

Die Autorinnen danken

Michaela Theuerer

Die Aufnahme in den Anhang zur Schulbuchliste für die 4. Klasse HS und AHS im Unterrichtsgegenstand Englisch wurde vom Bundesministerium für Bildung, Wissenschaft und Kultur mit BMBWK 5.018/157-V/9/2005 vom 24. Februar 2006 empfohlen.
Schulbuchnummer 130117

www.ggverlag.at

ISBN 978-3-7074-0761-7
Schulbuchnummer 130117

1. Auflage 2005, Nachdruck 2012 (1,07)
Illustrationen: Elena Obermüller
Printed by Litotipografia Alcione, Lavis-Trento, über Agentur Dalvit, D-85521 Ottobrunn

Vorwort

Liebe Schülerin! Lieber Schüler!

Du hältst ein Übungsbuch in der Hand, das dir helfen soll, auf einfache Art und Weise in Englisch aufzusteigen.
Wahrscheinlich bist du in Englisch nicht so gut und musst daher zusätzlich zu deinen Schulaufgaben noch etwas tun. Vielleicht hat dir deine Lehrerin/dein Lehrer empfohlen, zu Hause zu lernen. Vielleicht fürchtest du sogar, heuer durchzufallen.
Mit „Aufsteigen in Englisch 4" ist das Üben ganz leicht! Der wichtigste Stoff der Unterstufe ist hier zusammengefasst.
In sehr einfachen Merksätzen und mit leicht verständlichen Kurzinformationen werden dir hier die wichtigsten Kapitel des Stoffes der 4. Klasse HS/AHS und NMS erklärt.
Es folgen Übungen in unterschiedlichen Schwierigkeitsgraden. Du kannst diese Übungen auch allein machen. Sie sind im Lösungsteil genau ausgearbeitet.
Wir wünschen dir viel Erfolg beim Aufsteigen in Englisch!

Liebe Eltern!

Sie halten ein Übungsbuch in der Hand, das die Englischkenntnisse Ihres Kindes mit einfachen Übungen und leicht verständlichen Merksätzen verbessern kann.
Das Buch ist auf die Lernziele, die Ihr Kind in der 4. Klasse HS/AHS und NMS erreichen soll, abgestimmt. Dieser Stoff wird mit Abschluss der Unterstufe für die Berufsausbildung oder in weiterführenden Schulen vorausgesetzt.
Es ist so aufgebaut, dass ein Selbststudium durch die Lernenden möglich ist. Hilfe und Interesse seitens einer Lernbetreuung ist aber immer gut!

Zum Umgang mit diesem Buch:
Jedes Kapitel wird mit einem einfachen Theorieteil eingeleitet. In schrittweisen Erklärungen und mit leicht verständlichen Kurzinformationen werden die theoretischen Voraussetzungen für die folgenden Übungen gelegt.
Die Übungen werden immer genau beschrieben.
Im Lösungsteil ist jede Übung (bis auf einige wenige Vorübungen für Texte am Ende des Buches) komplett ausgearbeitet. Die Beispiele sind so gewählt, dass sie eindeutig zu lösen sind und das Kind eine sichere Kontrolle hat.
Das Übungsbuch kann auch als Nachschlagewerk bei etwaigen Fragen zur Grammatik eingesetzt werden.

Bei Schülern mit Schwierigkeiten in Englisch kann durch das Hinführen zum Verständnis von Strukturen und Zusammenhängen sowie durch gezieltes Üben eine merkliche Verbesserung erreicht werden.
Dieser Übungsband hilft dabei!

Viel Erfolg für Ihr Kind wünschen ihnen

Astrid Berger und Gabriele Broniowski

Symbolerklärung

Ü 1

Übungsaufgabe
Die Übungen sind fortlaufend nummeriert, sodass du sie auch im Lösungsteil für die Kontrolle leicht wiederfindest.
Einige Übungen kannst du im Buch erledigen (Ausfüllen von Lückentexten, Einsetzen in Spalten, Unterstreichen im Text), für andere Übungen ist es aber ratsam, wenn du dir ein kleines Übungsheft anlegst.

In einem solchen Kästchen findest du **wichtige Kurzinformationen** und **leicht verständliche Erklärungen** zum jeweiligen Thema.

Wichtiger Merksatz! Guter Tipp! Merke dir das gut!

Dem Buch ist ein Lösungsheft beigelegt, in dem alle Übungen dieselbe Nummer haben wie im Buch und genau ausgearbeitet sind.

Inhalt

some – any

Das Wesentliche über die Verwendung von **some** und **any** und deren Zusammensetzungen wie **something/anything**, **somebody/anybod**y, oder **somewhere/anywhere** weißt du schon. (Aufsteigen in Englisch 2, S. 9–12)

Hier das Wichtigste nochmals ganz kurz zur Erinnerung:

- **Some** verwendest du für gewöhnlich in **Aussagesätzen.**
- **Any** verwendest du für gewöhnlich in **Fragen und Verneinungen.**
- Als verneint gelten auch Sätze, in denen **hardly**, **never** oder **without** steht. Auch hier verwendest du **any.**
  *I've **never** seen **anything** more beautiful.*
  *There were **hardly any** people I knew.*
  *I'm sure you can do it **without any** problem.*
- Ist der Fragesatz eine **Bitte**, dann verwendest du **some.**
  *Could I have **some** milk, please?*
- Ist der Fragesatz eigentlich ein **Angebot**, dann verwendest du **some.**
  Would you like some cake?
- Du verwendest **any** häufig in Verbindung mit **if.**
- **Any** kann in Aussagesätzen irgendein/e bzw. jede/r/s Beliebige bedeuten.

Ü 1 **Setze die richtigen Formen von"some" oder "any" bzw. deren Zusammensetzungen ein:**

1. The minister didn't give the journalists ________________ detailed information.
2. We found out __________ very interesting facts when we talked to the police officer.
3. I can't tell you ________________ about the meeting.
4. Ms Brown will be with you in a minute. She is ________________ in the building.
5. I've never met __________________ who spoke Chinese.
6. Would you like __________________ to drink?
7. Getting there is not difficult. ________________ can tell you the way.
8. The thieves had stolen everything. There we were without ___________ money or credit cards.
9. __________________ must tell Joseph to be there on time. Otherwise he will miss the train.

10. Can you tell me ________________ about the people who want to buy our firm? Sorry, I don't know ________________. But Bill might know ________________ about them.
11. ________________ people think they can get away with everything.
12. I've no idea where I left my keys. They could be ________________.
13. Sally's grandmother spent everything on travelling. There was hardly ________________ money left when she died.
14. Yesterday Sandra bought ________________ interesting books in a little bookshop ________________ near the church.
15. We didn't see ________________ who could tell us ________________ about the history of the castle.
16. ________________ people always see the negative side of things.
17. I can't find ________________ in my room. I think I will have to do ________________ about the chaos there.
18. Where are my glasses? I must have left them ________________ in the garden.
19. Are there ________________ interesting new films I should see?
20. It doesn't matter what T-shirt you buy. ________________ colour will do.
21. You don't have to call a specialist. ________________ can do it.
22. ________________ is bothering her. I just don't know what.
23. Can I borrow ________________ of your pencils?
24. I know that you don't want to unload the dishwasher, but ________________ has to do it.
25. I'm sorry I haven't been able to find ________________ of the books you wanted.
26. There is ________________ on TV about the life of gorillas.
27. I can't find our cat Mia, she must be hiding ________________ in the cellar.
28. I would like to know ________________ about the history of this place.
29. We can show you ________________ of our orchids. They are very special. You hardly find ________________ of their kind in Europe.
30. Andrew must know ________________ about the accident, he was there when it happened.

Comparison

Comparison of adjectives

Du erinnerst dich sicher an die Steigerung der Adjektive:

- **„-er“ und „-est“**
  (einsilbige Adjektive und zweisilbige, die auf „-y“, „-r“, „-le“, und „-ow“ enden)
- **„more“ und „most“**
  (zweisilbige Adjektive, die nicht auf „-y“, „-r“, „-le“, und „-ow“ enden, und drei- und mehrsilbige Adjektive)
- **unregelmäßige Steigerung**

good	better	best
bad	worse	worst
much →	more	most
many →	more	most
little (wenig)	less	least
little (klein)	smaller	smallest
near	nearer →	nearest (räumlich am nächsten)
near	nearer →	next (in der Reihenfolge am nächsten)

Comparison of adverbs

- Adverbs, die auf „-ly“ enden, werden mit **more** und **most** gesteigert.

Yesterday it rained **more heavily** than today.
Could you try to work **more quietly**, please?

- **Unregelmäßige Steigerung:**

well	better	best
badly	worse	worst

Ü 2

Vervollständige jeden Satz mit einer Steigerungsform und eventuell nötigen anderen Wörtern:

1. Mount Everest is ______________________ mountain in the world. (high)
2. Trains don't go ________________________ planes. (fast)
3. Last Sunday was one of ________________________ days of the year. (cold)
4. My brother is ___________________ person I know. (lazy)
5. I think this film is much ______________________ the other one. (good)
6. We were really surprised. The book was _____________________________ we had expected. (interesting)
7. Andy and Nick are the same height. Andy is ____________________ Nick. (tall)
8. The last test was difficult but this one is _____________________. (easy)
9. This is _______________________ holiday we have ever had. (bad)
10. The CD is ____ the DVD. (expensive)
11. London has ________________________ inhabitants ____________ Vienna. (many)
12. These two T-shirts are the same price. The blue one is _______________ _______________________ the red one. (expensive)
13. The hummingbird is ________________________ bird we know. (small)
14. I have worked so hard. Look, my text is even _____________________ Sarah's. (long)
15. I don't understand why I have to be home ____________________ my sister. (early)

Ü 3

Vervollständige den zweiten Satz so, dass er das Gleiche bedeutet wie der erste:

Example:

Sarah learns faster than Ann.

Ann does not learn as fast as Sarah.

1. Andrew drank less than Simon.

   Andrew didn't ____.
2. Nobody is slower than Paul.

   Paul is ____.
3. This is as much as I can do.

   I can't ____.
4. You haven't bought as many books as Tim.

   Tim has ____.

5. This book is more interesting than "Harry Potter and the Prisoner of Azkaban".

   "Harry Potter and the Prisoner of Azkaban" is ______________________.

6. John learns more than Tim.

   Tim doesn't ______________________________________.

7. I don't know as many people as my brother.

   My brother knows ____________________________________.

8. Nobody is as clever as Sandra.

   Sandra is ____.

9. The weather is much better today than yesterday.

   Yesterday the weather was _____________________________.

10. Nobody in our school is more intelligent than Sean.

    Sean is ____ in our school.

11. We haven't bought as many books as you have.

    You've bought ______________________________________.

12. Phil talks a lot faster than Ann does.

    Ann doesn't talk ____________________________________.

13. Could you not drive so fast, please?

    Could you drive _____________________________________?

14. Skiing is not as exciting as bungee jumping.

    Bungee jumping is ___________________________________.

15. The book I'm reading now is more interesting than the last one.

    The last book I read was _____________________________.

16. Tina is the tallest girl in our class.

    Everyone else in our class is ___________________________.

17. They didn't pay more than we did.

    They paid just as_____________________________________.

18. Nobody is a better tennis player than Peter.

    Peter is ____.

19. I don't like music as much as my best friend.

    My best friend likes __________________________________.

20. Bill Gates is richer than the Queen of England.

    The Queen of England is ______________________________.

Ü 4 Vervollständige die folgenden Sätze:

1. My MP3-player is __________ good ___________ yours. They are both the same.
2. My father's car was ________ expensive _____________ my brother's.
3. This is one of the ________________ famous buildings in Vienna.
4. Sarah is taller _____________ her friend Mary but she is not __________ tall __________ her brother.
5. Everyone ate more _____________ Sarah.
6. This is a terrible film. It's one of the ______________ (bad) films I know.
7. You are a careless driver. You should drive __________ carefully.
8. It doesn't matter what you buy. This present is ________ expensive ___________ that one.
9. Andrew works _________ hard _________ all the other students in his class.
10. I think a holiday in the mountains is ___________ relaxing than sightseeing in a big city. But a holiday at the seaside is ___ _____ relaxing holiday of all.

Ü 5 Ergänze die fehlenden Steigerungsformen und füge auch die Wörter ein, die sonst noch fehlen:

cheap, easy, bad, handsome, lazy, warm, boring, nice, good, happy

1. Norway is too cold in autumn. I want to go to Italy where it is ____________.
2. Yesterday I met the _________________ man I have ever seen. It was great!
3. This exercise is much too difficult, let's do an ______________ one.
4. This is the ______________ coffee I have ever tasted. I'll never come to this coffeeshop again.
5. I can't afford these tickets. Let's get ______________ ones.
6. Sandra is the _______________ person I know. She spends most of her time sitting there doing nothing.
7. I don't think this is a good MP3 player. I want a ________________ one.
8. I thought I was going to fall asleep. It was really _________________ ___________ book I know.
9. When Mona passed her final exam, it was the _______________ day in her life.
10. I really like Mary! She is the _______________ person I know.

Adverb

Ein Adverb **bestimmt ein Verb, ein Adjektiv oder ein anderes Adverb** näher.

- **Adverb** bestimmt **Verb** näher:

  The students [listened] [carefully].
  Verb (listened), *Adverb* (carefully)

- **Adverb** bestimmt **Adjektiv** näher:

  Sandra and Paul are [terribly] [nice] people.
  Adverb (terribly), *Adjektiv* (nice)

- **Adverb** bestimmt anderes **Adverb** näher:

  I think she did it [really] [nicely].
  Adverb (really), *Adverb* (nicely)

Bildung des Adverbs

1. Meist durch Anhängen von -ly an das Adjektiv

nice	–	nicely	
loud	–	loudly	
slow	–	slowly	
quiet	–	quietly	
sad	–	sadly	
terrible	–	terribly	*Bei Wörtern, die auf -le enden, fällt beim Anhängen von -ly das „e" aus.*
horrible	–	horribly	
possible	–	possibly	
happy	–	happily	*Beachte, dass aus dem „y" ein „i" wird!*
angry	–	angrily	
easy	–	easily	
beautiful	–	beautifully	*Vergiss nicht auf die Verdoppelung des „l"!*
careful	–	carefully	

2. Adjektive, die auf -ly enden

Wenn das Adjektiv auf -ly endet, dann macht es natürlich keinen Sinn, noch ein -ly anzuhängen. Hier muss man umschreiben.

friendly	in a friendly way/manner
silly	in a silly way/manner
lovely	in a lovely way/manner

3. Andere Formen

good – well

„well" ist aber auch ein Adjektiv mit der Bedeutung „gesund".

Hi Liz, how are you today? Thanks, I'm very well.

fast – fast
long – long

4. Adverbs mit verschiedener Bedeutung

- fair → fair (= fair)
- fair → fairly (= ziemlich)
- hard → hard (= hart)
- hard → hardly (= kaum)
- near → near (= nahe)
- near → nearly (= beinahe)
- late → late (= spät)
- late → lately (= in letzter Zeit)
- pretty → pretty (= ziemlich)
- pretty → prettily (hübsch)

5. Verben, nach denen kein Adverb steht

Wenn du bestimmte Verben näher beschreiben willst, dann verwendest du trotzdem das Adjektiv. Diese Verben sind:

- look (aussehen), sound (klingen), smell (riechen), taste (schmecken), feel (fühlen)

"Jenny, you **look beautiful** today!"
I always **feel terrible** before an exam.

- Auch alle **Formen von „to be"** werden mit einem **Adjektiv** verwendet.
  "The baby **is so quiet**. Are you sure she is okay?"
- Verben, die auf Deutsch **„werden"** bedeuten: become, grow, get, turn
  "If you don't stop now, I'll **get angry**!"
- seem (= scheinen)
  She **seems nice** but she is a difficult person.
- remain (= bleiben)
  Paul **remained calm** in that awful situation.

6. Einige Ausdrücke zum Merken

to speak loud(ly)
That's real(ly) cool! — *Besonders im American English ohne -ly.*
Take it easy!
to guess right/wrong
to answer right/wrong

Ü 6

Setze die richtigen Wörter ein, Adjektiv oder Adverb:

interesting, happy, extremely, terrible, hardly, fast, quite, terribly, ill, hard, exciting, really

1. I was so tired that I ______________ noticed that Paul was leaving.
2. Mother was very ______________ when she heard that Tina had passed the exam.
3. I think she is an ____________ person. The stories she tells are so ______________.
4. Paul felt ________________ on the morning after the party. He had had too much to drink.
5. Tony forgot to do his homework again. He is an ________________ lazy boy.
6. My father worked very ______________ and was given some extra money by his boss.
7. I am surprised that you bought the MP3-player. I think it is ________________ expensive.
8. It's not a book I would read again, but it's _____________ good.
9. Father was driving too ______________ and was stopped by the police. He got ________________ angry because it was the second time that week.
10. My best friend is very ______________ and has to stay in bed for a week.

Ü 7

Ergänze die richtigen Formen, Adjektiv oder Adverb:

1. Stop that noise or I'll get very ________________. (angry)
2. If the machine does not work, you'll get your money back ________________________ (automatic).
3. The noise stopped ______________________ . (unexpected)
4. This is such a __________________ (beautiful) place!
5. There is an _____________________ (extreme) interesting film on TV, do you want to see it?
6. Where is that __________________ (nice) man who helped me with the luggage yesterday?
7. You could _________________ (easy) pass the exam if you worked _________________ (hard).
8. She touched the baby very _________________ (gentle) because she didn't want to hurt the little girl.
9. These are ________________ (good) seats, I can see the stage very _________________ (good).
10. I don't know Mr Brown very _______________ (good) but he seems very ________________ (nice).
11. Why does your coffee always taste so _______________ (awful)? I've told you often enough how to make it!
12. Where did you buy this beautiful shirt? It must have been __________ (terrible) expensive.
13. Your little son is such a _____________ (polite) boy, he always greets me __________ ___________________________ (friendly).
14. Don't make so much noise, you know how grandma hates it when you talk so ___________________ (loud).
15. This car is ___________________ (surprising) cheap, what's wrong with it?
16. Why does she always look so __________________ (unhappy)?
17. It's _______________ (pretty) late, let's go home now.
18. The roads were ___________________________ (terrible) busy yesterday. I ___________________ (near) missed the beginning of the play because I was in a traffic jam.

19. I opened the door ______________ (slow) because I had heard a ________________ (strange) noise.
20. What has happened to Tom and Sandra? We _____________ (hard) ever meet them.
21. Susan, you look ______________ (terrific)! What a ____________ (nice) coat!
22. I really enjoyed yesterday's party. Time passed so _______________ (quick).
23. Last year there was a ________________ (terrible) earthquake. Hundreds of people were _________________ (bad) injured.
24. It is _________________ (perfect) alright for you to leave early.
25. My best friend usually feels______________ (nervous) before exams.
26. Do you know Christine? She learns new languages ______________ (incredible) ______________ (quick).
27. His house is at the end of Wandsworth Road. You will find it ________ (easy).
28. You should ask Ann to help you. She speaks English _______________ (fluent).
29. What's the matter with Peter? He is _________________ (unusual) quiet.
30. I'm glad Tim looks _______________ (fit) again. He was _________________ (serious) ill last year.
31. It was raining ________________ (heavy) when we left the theatre.
32. I had an accident last week. Fortunately, the car was only ________________ (slight) damaged.
33. I think this is an __________________ (extreme) difficult exercise.
34. There is ________________ (hard) any snow in the mountains this year.
35. I like your new trousers. They look _______________ (good) on you.
36. Don't ask me about the food at Paul's party! The soup smelt so _________________ (horrible) that I didn't even want to taste it.
37. When the doctor finally arrived everybody was sitting _____________ (patient) in the waiting room.
38. Karen was _______________ (terrible) upset when I saw her yesterday. Do you know what happened?
39. Who is that ________________ (handsome) guy over there? He can't be Monica's boy-friend. She is such a _____________ (boring) person.
40. We stayed in a _________________ (nice) hotel which was ___________________ (reasonable) cheap.

Past perfect

Bildung

Subjekt + had + 3. Form des Verbs

Verwendung

Wenn du etwas erzählst, so geschieht das meist in der Erzählzeit, der past tense. Manchmal willst du aber über Handlungen und Ereignisse sprechen, die **vor der Erzählzeit** geschehen sind. Dann musst du **past perfect** verwenden.

I came home in the evening. When I turned on the lights I realised that somebody **had broken** into the house.
(Jemand war eingebrochen, BEVOR ich nach Hause kam.)

Yesterday I wanted to eat a yoghurt in the morning but there were no yoghurts left. **I had eaten** the last yoghurt the day before.
(Ich hatte das letzte Joghurt gegessen, BEVOR ich gestern eines haben wollte.)

After **she had lost** her credit card Sarah went to the police.
(Sie ging zur Polizei, NACHDEM sie ihre Kreditkarte verloren hatte.)

Past perfect verwendest du auch in der Indirekten Rede (Reported speech). Siehe Seite 48.
Auch in If-sentences bei Conditional III verwendest du Past perfect. Siehe Seite 20.

Ü 8

Past perfect or past tense:

1. By the time the firemen ____________________ (arrive), the fire ______________________________ (already/go out).
2. When Adam ____________________ (meet) Eve at the party he ________________ (think) that he ____________________ (see) her somewhere before.
3. After he ______________________ (buy) the computer he discovered that it ________________________ (not have) a DVD writer.
4. I went to the post office to ask about my parcel, but they _________________ (say) that it _________________________ (still not arrive).
5. The Vikings ________________________ (sail) to North America a thousand years ago.

6. After she ________________ (look) at the new dress for ages, she ________________ (ask) how much it cost.
7. When the Millers ________________ (save) enough money, they ________________ (go) on holiday.
8. When Mike couldn't find his keys, he was sure he ________________ (lose) them.
9. First I ________________ (study) for an hour, then I ________________ (go) for a walk.
10. I ________________ (arrive) at the train station at 7:50, just before the train ________________ (leave).
11. The police suspected that the burglar ________________ (get) into the house through the garage.
12. The team ________________ (celebrate) after they ________________ (win) the final match.
13. If I ________________ (buy) more milk, we would have had enough for breakfast.
14. They ________________ (get) lost because they ________________ (forget) to take a map with them.
15. I feel sick. I wish I ________________ (not eat) so much.
16. When she came home she ________________ (notice) that she ________________ (forget) to lock the door. Thank God nobody ________________ (break) in.
17. Pam told us that she ________________ (win) a trip to London.
18. By the time I got to the phone it ________________ (stop) ringing.
19. When they came to the airport, they ________________ (be informed) that their plane ________________ (be delayed).
20. When I ________________ (be) on holiday last summer I ________________ (go) to the beach every day.
21. If I ________________ (know) that you were ill, I would have visited you.
22. They had to build a new house because the tsunami ________________ (destroy) their old one.
23. They could not cross the river because the flood ________________ (wash) away the bridge.
24. We ________________ (get) up early because we ________________ (have) to be at the airport at 6 o'clock.

If-sentences

Bedingungssätze

Conditional 0

(Häufig unter Conditional I zu finden)

Manchmal willst du ausdrücken, **welche Folgen eine Handlung im Allgemeinen hat.** Zum Beispiel in den folgenden Sätzen:

If I don't do my homework in the afternoon, my **mum gets** angry. *(Das ist immer so.)*
If you steal something, **you are** a thief. *(Das ist eine allgemeine Feststellung.)*
My **mother takes** me to the doctor if **I don't feel** okay. *(Das geschieht immer.)*

Hier beschreibst du eine Situation, die im Allgemeinen so abläuft. Du sprichst über die Folgen einer Handlung im Allgemeinen. Es handelt sich nicht um einen besonderen Fall. Wenn du die obigen Sätze anschaust, dann siehst du, dass du folgende Zeiten verwendest:

<u>If + Subjekt + present simple</u>	<u>Subjekt + present simple</u>
If-Satz	**Hauptsatz**

Conditional I

Manchmal möchtest du aber auch ausdrücken, **welche Folgen** eine ganz bestimmte Handlung, ein ganz bestimmtes Geschehen, ein ganz bestimmter Zustand haben werden.

If you don't stop that noise, **I'll** get really angry!
If the weather is good, we'll climb Mount Owen tomorrow.
I'll never do it again if **you forgive me** now.

Hier beschreibst du die Folgen, die eine **ganz bestimmte** Handlung haben wird. In einem solchen Fall verwendest du folgende Zeiten:

<u>If + Subjekt + present simple</u>	<u>Subjekt + will + Infinitiv (= will-future)</u>
If-Satz	**Hauptsatz**

Conditional II

Manchmal sprichst du über **unwahrscheinliche Situationen**. Du willst ausdrücken, **was als Folge einer bestimmten Situation geschehen könnte**.

If I had a lot of money, I **would buy** a Ferrari.
Du hast aber leider nicht viel Geld.

If you were a good friend, you **would help** me.
Scheinbar bist du aber kein guter Freund.

They **would tell** me **if they knew** the answer.
Leider wissen sie die Antwort aber nicht.

She would not go there **if she was** a clever girl.
Sie scheint aber kein kluges Mädchen zu sein.

Du verwendest also folgende Zeiten:

If + Subjekt + past simple	Subjekt + would + Infinitiv
If-Satz	**Hauptsatz**

Achtung: Im If-Satz steht in der Regel kein would!

Manchmal kommt es auch vor, dass jemand **"if I were"**, oder **"if he/she were"** verwendet. Diese Formen sind sehr korrektes Englisch, werden aber in der Alltagssprache eher selten gebraucht.

Conditional III

Es gibt Fälle, in denen du sagen möchtest, was unter bestimmten Bedingungen in der Vergangenheit geschehen hätte können, aber nicht geschehen ist.

If you had arrived in time, you **would not have missed** the train.
Du warst aber nicht rechtzeitig dort und hast daher den Zug versäumt.

If Liz had talked to Sam, he **would have been** so happy.
Sie hat aber nicht mit ihm gesprochen, daher war er nicht glücklich.

If + Subjekt + past perfect	Subjekt + would have + 3. Form d. Verbs
If-Satz	**Hauptsatz**

Vorsicht! Manchmal sprichst du auch darüber, was für Folgen Dinge, die in der Vergangenheit geschehen hätten können, auf die Gegenwart haben könnten. Du solltest diesen Bedeutungsunterschied beachten. Je nachdem, was du sagen willst, verwendest du im Hauptsatz die entsprechende Zeitform.

If I had been at the concert yesterday, I **would have seen** a super stage show.
*Ich habe die Bühnenshow **gestern** nicht gesehen.* ⟶ would have + 3. Form

If I had been at the concert, I **would be** very tired **now**.
*Ich bin **jetzt** nicht müde.* ⟶ would + Nennform

If-sentences – Conditional III

Ü 9

Ergänze die Verben in der richtigen Zeit:

1. I ____________________ (buy) that dress if it had not been so expensive.
2. If we ____________________ (have) some bread, we could have made some sandwiches.
3. If he had had time, he ____________________ (help) us move into our new house.
4. You would have lost your job if the kids ____________________ (misbehave = sich schlecht benehmen) on the school trip.
5. If I had met George in the street, I ____________________ (not recognize) him.
6. The photograph would have been better if it ____________________ (take) during the day.
7. If he ____________________ (offer) me the job I would have taken it.
8. I ____________________ (pick) you up at the station if you had called me the day before.
9. The burglar would have broken in, if the alarm system ____________________ (not frighten) him away.
10. If they had not spent all their money on expensive trips they ____________________ ____________________ (can/buy) a bigger house.
11. You would not have passed the exam if Mona ____________________ (not study) with you.
12. If it had not been so late we ____________________ (walk) home after the party.

13. If she ____________________ (know) about his problems she would have tried to help him.
14. If you had not pulled me back I ____________________ (fall) off the cliff.
15. If they had not sent a search-party for the little boy he ____________________ (die) in the snow.
16. We would have crashed into the wall if you ____________________ (not step) on the brake in time.
17. If she had not won the lottery she ____________________ (cannot/spend) a year in Australia.
18. If we ____________________ (run) a bit faster we would have caught the train.
19. If I had known you were there I ____________________ (look) for you in the crowd.
20. If you ____________________ (leave) a message on the answering machine I would have called you back.
21. He ____________________ (not become) sick if he had not eaten so much.
22. If you ____________________ (read) the book you would have been able to answer the teacher's questions.
23. If they had told me about the meeting I ____________________ (come).
24. If he ____________________ (book) a flight in February he could have gone to Florida in June. Now it's too late.
25. If you had listened to me you ____________________ (not get) into trouble.
26. If you ____________________ (contact) me I could have told you about the change in plans.
27. We ____________________ (get) lost if the weather had not changed.
28. If he ____________________ (not miss) the train he would have died in the explosion.
29. If we had stayed at the party a little bit longer we ____________________ (meet) the famous writer.
30. If the weather ____________________ (be) nice we could have gone to the beach.

Conditionals I + II + III

Ü 10

Ergänze die Verben in der richtigen Zeit:

1. If I had known you were in hospital I ______________________ (visit) you.
2. If he ______________ (not be) so lazy, he would get better grades.
3. If I ______________ (know) that the plane was delayed (= verspätet), I would have left an hour later.
4. If she practised more, she _________________ (play) the saxophone better.
5. If you read more books in English, your English __________________ (improve).
6. If they had not told me about the film, I ______________________ (miss) it.
7. I would say she is happy if I __________________________ (not know) better.
8. If you ____________________ (not lie) to me before, I would have believed your story.
9. If Pamela hurries, she _______________ (not be) late.
10. If Sam ______________ (have) a bike, he would ride it to school.
11. If I had listened to the weather forecast, I ______________________ (not go) out.
12. If Margaret _______________ (take) her medicine regularly, she will get better soon.
13. If you _________________________ (not tell) me to stay out of the sun, I would have got sunburnt.
14. If you feel dizzy, ______________ (stop) taking the pills.
15. Your English _________________ (improve) rapidly if you practise every day.
16. If David __________________ (not live) so close to the school, he would have to get up earlier.
17. If Miriam had written a shopping list, she ________________________ (not forget) to buy some milk for breakfast.
18. If you ______________ (want) to come to the beach with us, I will ask my dad if it is okay.
19. Everybody in my class passed the final exam. If I ______________ (be) the teacher, I would be very proud.
20. If I ______________________ (turn) right at the post office, I would not have lost my way.
21. If you change your mind, _____________ (give) me a call.

22. If you _________________ (drop) the glass, it will break.
23. If they _________________________ (arrive) earlier, they would have got a better seat.
24. If the author of the Harry Potter books ___________________________ (not find) a publisher (= Verleger), she would not have become a rich woman.
25. If you ________________ (not be) careful and ______________ (break) the eggs, there will be a mess in the kitchen.
26. If we were late for class, our teacher __________________ (be) very angry.
27. If you ____________________ (not turn) down the volume of the TV, you will wake up the neighbours.
28. If Columbus had not tried to reach India by ship, he ______________________________ ____ (not discover) America.
29. Jack lost his wallet and he never got it back. If I found somebody's wallet, I ______________________ (take) it to the police station.
30. When it rains, the children usually __________________ (play) inside.
31. If our team __________________________ (score) more goals, we would have won the match.
32. If he had more money, he _________________ (pay) for you too.
33. There is a "No Parking" sign. If you __________________ (leave) the car here, the police will give you a parking ticket.
34. If people used bikes instead of cars, there ____________________ (not be) so much pollution.
35. The train station is not far away. If you __________________ (follow) this path, it will take you to the train station.
36. If I had not left my umbrella at home, I ___________________________ (not get) wet.
37. If I ever win the lottery, I _____________________ (share) the money with you.
38. If I _______________ (be) a famous pop star, people would probably recognize me in the street.
39. If you don't have any money, _________________ (get) a job.
40. If she ______________________________ (realize) you were tired, she would not have asked you to go for a walk with her.

ing oder Infinitiv

Es gibt Verben, auf die meistens eine ing-Form folgt, andere, auf die meist der Infinitiv folgt.

Einige Verben, auf die oft ein Infinitiv folgt

afford (sich leisten)
agree (zustimmen)
appear (scheinen)
ask (bitten)
attempt (versuchen)
choose (wählen)
decide (beschließen)
expect (erwarten)
forget (vergessen)
happen (zufällig)
help (helfen)
hope (hoffen)
used to (pflegte/n etwas zu tun)
intend (beabsichtigen)
learn (lernen)
mean (beabsichtigen)
need (brauchen, müssen)
offer (anbieten)
prepare (vorbereiten)
pretend (vortäuschen)
promise (versprechen)
refuse (sich weigern, verweigern)
seem (scheinen)
want (wollen)
wish (wünschen)

I can't **afford to buy** such an expensive car.
They **hoped to find** a cheap hotel.
We **agreed to meet** again in the evening.
Paul **pretended not to be** interested in Sheila.
Susan **promised to help** them with the job.
She **refused to leave** before she had spoken to the boss.
Carol **offered to pick** me up at the station.
We **decided not to wait** any longer.

Einige Verben, auf die oft eine ing-Form folgt

- admit (zugeben)
- avoid (vermeiden)
- can't help (nicht anders können)
- can't stand (nicht ertragen können)
- consider (in Erwägung ziehen)
- deny (leugnen)
- detest (verabscheuen)
- dislike (nicht mögen)
- enjoy (genießen, Spaß haben an)
- feel like (Lust haben auf)
- finish (aufhören, beenden)
- imagine (sich vorstellen)
- it's no use (es hat keinen Sinn)
- keep (weitermachen)
- mind (es macht etwas aus)
- miss (vermissen)
- postpone (verschieben)
- practise (üben)
- resist (widerstehen)
- risk (riskieren)
- suggest (vorschlagen)

Can you **imagine living** in that small village in the middle of nowhere?
I **avoid walking** through the park at night.
Sam looked so funny, I **couldn't help laughing**.
Would you **consider moving** to Rome if you were offered a job there?
They **postponed travelling** to India because of the earthquake.
I wouldn't **risk losing** my job because of such a stupid idea.
When I came home I **felt like spending** a quiet evening watching TV.
Don't stop now, just **keep going**!
Would you **mind opening** the window?

Einige Verben, auf die entweder ing-Form oder Infinitiv folgen kann

- can't bear (nicht ertragen können)
- begin (beginnen)
- continue (weitermachen)
- hate (hassen)
- like (mögen)
- love (lieben)
- prefer (vorziehen)
- regret (bedauern)
- remember (sich erinnern)
- see (sehen)
- start (beginnen)
- stop (aufhören)
- try (versuchen)

Bei den meisten dieser Verben macht es nicht viel Unterschied, ob du sie mit Infinitiv oder ing-Form verwendest.

Wenn du **would** mit **hate**, **like**, **love** oder **prefer** kombinierst, dann musst du aber auf jeden Fall den Infinitiv verwenden:

I **would like to** go to the cinema.
I'd prefer to stay at home.

Bei manchen dieser Verben gibt es allerdings einen Bedeutungsunterschied, je nachdem, ob sie mit Infinitiv oder ing-Form kombiniert werden:

1. remember + infinitive: sich erinnern, dass man etwas tun muss
   remember + ing-Form: sich an etwas erinnern, das schon passiert ist

   I must **remember to call** Andrew in the afternoon.
   I can't **remember putting** the folder there, can you?

2. stop + infinitive: eine Tätigkeit unterbrechen, um etwas anderes zu tun
   stop + ing-Form: mit einer Tätigkeit aufhören

   She **stopped to change** a tyre.
   Paul **stopped smoking** last year.

3. try + infinitive: sich bemühen etwas zu tun
   try + ing-Form: mit etwas experimentieren, um zu sehen, was passiert

   He **tried to solve** the problem but he couldn't.
   Have you ever **tried adding** more sugar to the mixture?

Im Falle von "like" ist es oft gleichgültig, welche Form du verwendest. Du kannst also sagen:

Paul **likes getting** up early. ODER Paul **likes to get up** early.

Im Britischen Englisch gibt es manchmal einen kleinen Bedeutungsunterschied, je nachdem, ob du like mit Infinitiv oder mit ing-form verwendest:

"like doing" drückt aus, dass ich etwas gern tue, genieße, es mir Spaß macht.

I like sailing. *Es macht mir Spaß, ich tue es gern.*

"like to do" drückt eher aus, dass man der Meinung ist, es sei richtig etwas zu tun.

I like to wash the dishes before I leave my flat in the morning.
Es macht mir nicht unbedingt Spaß, aber ich halte es für richtig es zu tun.

Die ing-Form des Zeitwortes wird immer nach **Präpositionen** (in, of, from, on, for, after, before ...) verwendet.

He got a medal **for swimming** a new world record.
After working in the garden, he slept well.
Always turn off the light **before leaving** the room.

Ausnahmen gibt es bei "to", das oft mit dem Infinitiv steht.
Aber: I am looking **forward to seeing** you.

Es gibt auch andere Wörter (keine Verben), die in Verbindung mit einer **ing-Form** verwendet werden:

when	**When travelling** in the desert, take enough water with you.
while	Tim always sang **while working** in the garden.

Ü 11 ing-Form oder Infinitiv?

1. He admitted to steal ________ (steal) the car.
2. My sister forgot to buy ________ (buy) milk.
3. The thief refused telling ________ (tell) the police where the money was.
4. They suggested to go ________ (go) to the cinema.
5. He promised ________________ (not forget) the book.
6. They seemed ________________ (be) very nice people.
7. He regrets ________________ (not study) harder when he was at school.
8. Has he decided what ________________ (give) her as a present?
9. Have you ever considered ________________ (look) for a new job?
10. I really miss ________________ (see) her every day in the morning.
11. Are you sure you can afford ________________ (buy) a new car?
12. Would you mind ________________ (pass) the salt?
13. He pretended ________________ (not know) us.
14. We asked him to stop ________________ (shout) but he took no notice.
15. Remind me ________________ (post) the letter on the way home.
16. The key is on the shelf. I remember ________________ (leave) it there.
17. Maria suggested ________________ (ask) Fred to help.
18. I really enjoyed ________________ (meet) your parents yesterday.
19. When you go shopping, please, don't forget ________________ (buy) the things on the list I gave you.
20. Anne loves ________________ (cook) but she hates ____________ (iron).
21. Sheila offered ________________ (look) after the kids while we were out.
22. She promised ________________ (come) earlier and help us.
23. I can't imagine Mr Chips ________________ (drive) a sports car.

24. People used ________________ (make) fire by __________________ (rub) two sticks together.

25. He surprised us all by ___________________ (go) away without __________________ (say) goodbye.

26. I can't help _______________________ (sneeze). I caught a cold yesterday from _______________________(sit) in a draught (= Zugluft).

27. I know my hair needs ________________________ (cut) but I never have the time __________________ (go) to the hairdresser's.

28. He made me _____________________ (repeat) the instructions ______________________ (make) sure that I understood what to do.

29. When he told me that everybody had made fun of him I couldn't help __________________ (feel) sorry for him.

30. When you see Tom, remember ___________________ (give) him my regards, won't you?

31. He tried ___________________ (reach) the shelf but he wasn't tall enough.

32. I often see her _____________________ (walk) towards the school after _____________________ (get) off the bus at the corner.

33. He translated the article without __________________ (use) a dictionary.

34. She stopped ___________________ (comfort) the crying child.

35. The doctor told me to stop ___________________ (smoke).

36. She apologized for ___________________ (borrow) my car without _____________________ (ask) my permission and promised never ______________________ (do) it again.

37. He keeps ___________________ (ask) me the time and I keep __________________ (tell) him ________________ (buy) himself a watch.

38. It is pleasant __________________ (sit) by the fire at night and __________________ (listen to) the wind ________________ (howl) outside.

39. We got tired of ____________________ (wait) for the weather ______________ (clear) and decided __________________ (set) out in the rain.

40. He wants __________________ (visit) his friends in Canada this year.

41. I enjoy __________________ (take) it easy on a Sunday afternoon.

42. My teacher wants me _________________ (work) harder.

43. Would you like ________________ (play) table tennis with me?
44. It's no use ________________ (tell) him to be punctual. He just doesn't care.
45. Last year we decided ________________ (travel) through Australia.
46. I don't mind ________________ (get) up early in summer.
47. My grandfather remembers ________________ (watch) the first quiz show on TV.
48. They tried ________________ (find) their way back to the dirt road, but they were lost in the desert.
49. Don't forget ________________ (give) her the invitation to your birthday party when you see her!
50. Jenny didn't finish ________________ (write) her essay until midnight.
51. You are always cold. I think you need ________________ (buy) a warm coat.
52. Peter enjoys ________________ (play) soccer with his friends.
53. I told Anna not to forget ________________ (lock) the door when she left the house.
54. Kim always likes ________________ (go) on holiday to hot countries.
55. You've still got that hiccup. Why don't you try ________________ (hold) your breath, or ________________ (drink) a glass of water?
56. Richard has always hated ________________ (live) in the country.
57. Dad tried ________________ (start) the car, but nothing happened.
58. She learned ________________ (use) sign language when she was still a toddler (= Kleinkind).
59. Ann prefers ________________ (read) to ________________ (play) computer games.
60. When the teacher came in some kids ignored him and continued ________________ (chat).
61. She appeared ________________ (be) really sorry for ________________ (have) lied to me.
62. Do you happen ________________ (know) the exact time?
63. Rose expects ________________ (win) the women's 100 m race.
64. Could you help me ________________ (carry) this into the house? It's extremely heavy.
65. I hope ________________ (see) you at my birthday party.

66. In the end, Cybill chose ________________ (leave) school and ________________ (become) an apprentice (= Lehrling).
67. Mona couldn't resist ________________ (tease) her brother.
68. Oliver, please go to the headmaster's/principal's office. He wishes ________________ (see) you.
69. What do you intend ______________ (do) about your bad marks/grades?
70. My aunt can't stand _______________ (drive) in big cities. She always gets very nervous.
71. My brother asked me _______________ (lend) him € 10 but I am not sure if I will ever get it back.
72. My dad can't risk ________________ (lose) his job. At his age it is very difficult to find a new job.
73. You should practise ________________ (read) aloud.
74. His friends agreed ____________ (meet) him at the shopping mall.
75. When the burglar attempted ________________ (break) into the house the alarm went off.
76. Bob and Celine don't get along very well but they can't really avoid ________________ (see) each other as they are in the same class.
77. Please remind me _______________ (ask) Alice for that wonderful strawberry cake recipe.
78. My grandma told me that she sometimes feels like _______________ (do) something forbidden.
79. Regina detests _______________ (fly) but going by plane is still the fastest way of _______________ (get) to London.
80. What I mean _______________ (say) is that if we don't hurry, we will miss the last bus.
81. The 14-year-old boy denied ________________ (beat) up his classmate.
82. I should have seen the car ________________ (come) but I was distracted.
83. They prepared ______________________ (leave) on the first day of the summer holidays/vacations.
84. You can't postpone ________________ (make) a decision any longer. You have to decide which school you want to go to.

85. Jason dislikes ________________ (argue = streiten). Arguments make him feel uncomfortable.

86. I can ask mum for anything because she can't bear ________________ (see) me cry.

87. What do you want ______________ (prove = beweisen) by __________________ (break) the rules?

88. When __________________ (check) in at the airport make sure you don't lose your passport.

89. They were attacked while ______________ (wait) for the train to Salzburg.

90. __________________ (become) successful is a lot of hard work.

Verbs + prepositions

Nach folgenden Verben und Präpositionen verwedest du immer die ing-Form.

to be accused of (angeklagt/beschuldigt werden wegen)
to apologize for (sich entschuldigen für)
to be afraid of (sich fürchten vor)
to be bored with (gelangweilt sein)
to be capable of (fähig sein)
to be fond of (etwas gerne haben)
to be good at/bad at (gut/schlecht sein bei etwas)
to be interested in (sich interessieren für)
to be keen on (etwas sehr gerne haben)
to be pleased about (froh sein über)
to be tired of (einer Sache müde sein)
to be used to (gewöhnt sein an)
to get used to (sich gewöhnen an)
to believe in (an etwas glauben)
to congratulate on (gratulieren zu)
to dream of (träumen von)
to feel like (Lust haben auf)
to forgive for (verzeihen)
to give up (etwas aufgeben/aufhören mit)
to go on (weitermachen mit)
to insist on (bestehen auf)
to keep on (weitermachen mit)
to know about (wissen über)
to look forward to (sich freuen auf)
to prevent somebody from (jemanden abhalten von etwas)
to put off (verschieben)
to succeed in (Erfolg haben bei)
to suspect of (verdächtigen)
to think of/about (nachdenken über)

Ü 12

Ergänze die Präpositionen und die ing-Formen:

1. Are you really interested ______________________ (buy) that house?
2. They couldn't leave earlier because he insisted ______________________ (have) a shower.
3. The police suspected the man ____________________ (be) a murderer.
4. I'm really looking forward ______________________ (travel) to France.
5. The man prevented her ______________________ (jump) out of the window.
6. His friend congratulated him ______________________ (pass) the exam.
7. Would you like a cigarette? No, thank you, I have given ________________ (smoke)!
8. Peter is interested _____________________ (learn) English. He needs it for his job.
9. She has been thinking ______________________ (look) for a new job.
10. Jason is putting on weight. He'll have to give _________________ (eat) snacks.
11. Heavy traffic prevented the bus ____________________ (arrive) on time.
12. Conny is looking forward ____________________ (spend) three weeks in Florida.
13. We tried to stop her, but she kept _______________ (talk).
14. I'm afraid I'm very bad __________________ (solve) maths problems.
15. The Johnsons had to put __________________ (move) to a new flat as Mr Johnson lost his job.
16. He apologized _______________________ (be) rude.
17. Last year the young tennis player succeeded ____________________ (win) all the major tournaments.
18. I am tired _______________________ (tell) you what to do. Think for yourself.
19. As she was bored ____________________ (watch) TV she decided to go for a walk with her dog.
20. He dreams ______________________ (become) a famous pop star.
21. The man was accused ________________________ (murder) his wife in cold blood.
22. I believe the police are on the wrong track. I don't think Adam is capable ___________________________ (hurt) anyone.
23. Paul can't get used _______________________ (get) up early. He is late every day.
24. Anna is not very keen _______________________ (ski). She prefers swimming and riding her bike.
25. Can you forgive me ___________________ (lie) to you? It won't happen again.

26. I firmly believe ______________________ (pack) my own suitcase. Then I can be relatively sure I have got everything I need for the trip.
27. Mona is invited to a party but as she is very tired she doesn't feel ________________________ (go) out tonight.
28. I'd like to know more _________________________________ (clone). I think it is an interesting topic.
29. The teacher told us to go _____________________ (read).
30. Tom is not very fond ______________________ (fly) but he loves going by train.
31. I don't think I could give ______________________ (eat) chocolate. I am a chocoholic.
32. Martin dreamed _________________________ (win) the lottery.
33. Are you interested _________________________ (do) sports?
34. I don't think you can put __________________________ (study) any longer. You have a test right after the Christmas holidays.
35. When Tanya got older she insisted ______________________ (have) her own room. She did not want to share a room with her brother any longer.

Phrasal verbs

Unter einem Phrasal verb versteht man ein „normales“ Verb, dem eine oder zwei Präpositionen folgen und das dadurch seine Bedeutung ändert. Manchmal ist die Bedeutung ähnlich wie beim Ursprungsverb, manchmal ist sie aber auch ganz anders.

Hier einige Beispiele für Phrasal verbs:

break down	zusammenbrechen, etwas niederreißen
bring up	aufziehen
care about	mögen, gern haben
care for	mögen, gern haben
carry on	weitermachen
check in/out	ein-/auschecken, an-/abmelden
clear up	aufhellen (Wetter)
close down	ein Geschäft/einen Betrieb für immer zusperren
drop out	aufgeben, aus einer Sache aussteigen
fill in	ausfüllen (Formular)
fix up	arrangieren
get along	auskommen mit
hang about	warten, herumlungern, sich herumtreiben
hang around	warten, herumlungern, sich herumtreiben
hang on	am Apparat bleiben (Telefon), warten
hold on	festhalten, warten
hurry up	sich beeilen
long for	sich sehnen nach
look after	aufpassen, sich kümmern um
look at	anschauen
look for	suchen
look forward to	sich freuen auf
look up	etwas nachschauen, nachschlagen
move in/out	einziehen/ausziehen
put on	anziehen (Kleidung)
put up with	sich abfinden mit, aushalten
set off	aufbrechen (zu einer Reise)
show off	angeben
sort out	aussortieren, ein Problem lösen
take care of	aufpassen, sich kümmern um
take off	starten (Flugzeug ...), ausziehen (Kleidung)
turn up	auftauchen, erscheinen, lauter drehen
turn on	einschalten
turn off	ausschalten

Ü 13 **Ergänze die folgenden Sätze mit einem der Phrasal verbs aus der Liste (in der korrekten Form):**

turn up	*look up*	*hurry up*	*fill in*	*sort out*	*break down*
hold on	*bring up*	*hold on*	*set off*	*close down*	*drop out*
move in	*take off*	*move out*	*put on*	*clear up*	*look after*
long for	*show off*	*look for*	*hang about*	*care for*	*get along*
turn on					

1. Yesterday we went to see our frinds in Linz. We decided to ________________ early in the morning to have enough time there.
2. I don't know what this word means. I'll have to __________________ it ____________ in the dictionary.
3. Paul and Sandra died in an accident. Now Paul's parents _________________ the children.
4. I must _____________________ my keys, I can't find them.
5. Our new house is almost finished. We want to ______________________________ in February.
6. Peter is a strange person. I hadn't heard from him for months and then he suddenly _______________________ yesterday evening.
7. The flat was locked. The police had to ______________________________ the door to get in.
8. Last week I wanted to buy something in the little shop in Parker Road. But when I arrived there I saw that it _______________________.
9. When we wanted to fly to the USA we had to ________________________ a lot of forms.
10. We went to the theatre yesterday evening and Jane _____________________ her little brother.
11. There was such chaos at the airport. Our plane _______________________ two hours late.
12. Why are you so angry? Don't you ____________________ me at all?
13. I wanted to take part in the bicycle race but it was too much for me. I _________________________ after 30 kilometres.
14. ____________________ a minute, I'll be with you as soon as possible.
15. I don't want to _______________________ for ages without anything to do.

16. I can't stand the busy city any longer. I ______________________ a quiet place somewhere in the country.
17. Mrs Anderson is a very competent person. She ___________________________ the problem in no time.
18. Yesterday was a terrible day. It was raining all morning. Only in the afternoon it finally __________________________.
19. I had no problem with Greg on our trip through Africa. We _________________ very well.
20. I hate Sam. He always __________________________ when he is with people he doesn't know well.
21. Could you ________________________, please! We don't want to miss our plane.
22. They are going to pull down our block of flats. We will have to _______________ very soon.
23. Jess, couldn't you _________________________ something more suitable for your sister's wedding?
24. Could you ________________________ the radio please? I want to listen to the news.
25. You want to talk to Ms Miller? Okay, _________________________, I'll try to get her for you.

Ü 14

Vervollständige die Sätze und verwende dazu die unten stehenden Satzteile:

1. Would you please fill ___________________________________
2. When did the sweet shop in your street close ______________________
3. I don't want the kids to hang ________________________________
4. Bill dropped _________________________________
5. We have to check __________________________________
6. Why does he have to show __________________________________
7. I think we will have to set ___________________________________
8. The plane took ____
9. She was longing _____________________________________
10. If you wait a minute, I will sort ________________________________
11. I will have to look ____

12. Ann told us to hurry ______________________________

13. They had to wait for the weather to clear ________________________

14. Don't look around and chat, carry ________________________

15. I didn't know what to put ______________________________

16. So this is your new apartment! Are you going to move __________________

17. We waited for an hour, but when nobody turned _______________________

18. I am not going to put _____________________________________

19. Could you hang ____

20. I really enjoyed our visit to the museum. I could have looked ________________ ____________________

21. Unfortunately, I couldn't see the end of the film. My father turned ____________ __________________________

22. Could you take care ____

23. I was looking ____

24. I don't care ____

in this form for me?
in this month?
the TV off because it was already very late.
up if we didn't want to miss the beginning of the play.
out of school when he was 16.
off from Heathrow Airport at 8 in the morning.
on for Sally's graduation ceremony.
of the children while I am getting our tickets?
on a moment, I'm trying to find the number for you.
down?
off when he is with his friends?
on working.
at the pictures for hours.
off early if we want to reach the summit (= Gipfel).
it out for you.
up with your behaviour (= Verhalten) any longer.
around all afternoon.
for a letter from her lover.
up his number in the phone book.
for opera.
up we went home.
for a parking space when I noticed that there was a new shop in Kennington Lane.
up before they could climb Mount Benson.
out in the morning.

Verb + Objekt + to + Infinitiv

Manchmal verwendet man im Englischen Strukturen, die sich vom Deutschen unterscheiden. Dazu gehört **Verb + Objekt + to + Infinitiv**. Diese Konstruktion wird mit folgenden Verben verwendet.

want	would like
ask	would love
expect	would hate
help	would prefer
beg	

I want you to listen carefully now.

Verb Objekt Infinitiv

She **asked me to stay** a little longer.
We **expect you to work** hard.
They **helped me to find** a good hotel.
She **begged me to help her** with the job.
I **would like you to be** there in time.
They **would love their daughter to become** a pianist.
I **would hate Tom to make** a fool of himself.
We **would prefer our children to attend** St. Mary's School.

Ü 15

Bilde vollständige Sätze! Beachte dabei, dass das Subjekt zum Objekt wird. Aus „I“ wird „me“, aus „he“ wird „him“ usw.

Sam/expect/everybody/admire/his work
Sam expects everybody to admire his work.

1. Peter/begged/his sister/not leave/him/alone/in the dark
2. They/wanted/I/do my homework/in the afternoon
3. Margaret/help/her best friend/redecorate her room
4. I/would like/my students/work harder
5. I/would prefer/my son/not play/with the children next door
6. Our teacher/want/we/listen/carefully
7. I/would hate/you/lose/your job/because of me
8. Mother/would love/we/move/to this town

9. Carol/expected/her brother/wait/for her/in front of the station
10. Mr Brown/want/his children/be home/in the evening
11. Sarah/would hate/I/talk/to her ex-husband
12. My brother/begged/I/not tell/my parents/his secret
13. Can/you/help/I/carry/this table/over to the window
14. I/would/prefer/Sam/work/from home
15. My parents/would hate/I/buy/such a flashy car
16. We/want/our teachers/treat us/in a friendly way
17. I/expect/my friends/help me/in a difficult situation
18. They/would like/we/move out/of the flat
19. Where/would you like/I/put/the flowerpot?
20. Our boss/begged/we/postpone/our holiday
21. Would/you/like/I/wait/for the taxi/with you?
22. My best friend/want/her husband/look for a better job.
23. Our mother/expect/we/pass/all exams
24. I/would hate/we/miss/the train
25. Mum/would prefer/we/come straight home/after the concert
26. I/would hate/my boy-friend/smoke/in the car
27. Carol/help/the children/find/a suitable present/for their mother
28. The teacher/wanted/we/learn/the new words
29. I/would love/Paul/spend/his holiday/with us
30. Charles/begged/his father/buy/him a new Gameboy

Präpositionen

Ü 16

Zur Wiederholung ergänze die fehlenden Präpositionen:

1. Were there many people _____ the concert?
2. Turn left _____ the traffic lights.
3. I usually go out _____ Friday evenings.
4. I'll see you ____ the morning.
5. They arrived ____ Christmas Day.
6. Will you be here ____ the weekend?
7. I usually go home ____ bus.
8. ____ Sunday I often get up ____ 9 o'clock.
9. Tom's grandmother died ____ 1979 ____ the age of 79.

10. I'm sorry, I can't find the book ___ the moment.

11. In the rush hour it's quicker to go ____ foot than _____ car.

12. Mozart was born ____ Salzburg ____ 1756.

13. I'm going out to do some shopping, I'll be back ____ half an hour.

14. I'll phone you _____ Tuesday morning ____ about 10 o'clock, okay?

15. It was quite a short book and easy to read. I read it ____ a day.

16. Do you fancy going to the cinema ____ Friday night?

17. Carol got married ___ 17, which is rather young to get married.

18. Hurry up! We got to go ____ five minutes.

19. I might not be at home ____ the morning. Can you phone me _____ the afternoon instead?

20. There are usually a lot of parties ____ New Year's Eve.

21. She likes to relax ____ weekends.

22. ___ Zack's party I saw a lot of good friends.

23. I haven't seen Anne for a few days. I last saw her ___ Tuesday.

24. Don't sit ___ that armchair. It's broken.

25. When we were ___ Italy, we spent a few days ____ Venice.

26. Vienna is situated ___ the river Danube.

27. Robert lives ___ a small village in the mountains. You can only get there ____ foot.

28. There's a report of the tennis match ___ page 7 of the newspaper.

29. Sue and David first met ____ Manchester four years ago.

30. When I go to Vienna I usually go ___ bus.

31. I'll be _______ work _________ 5:30.

32. He will talk ______ you ________ a few minutes.

33. Our flat is ______ the second floor _______ the building.

34. In Britain people drive ______ the left side.

35. I'm sorry, I can't find the book _____ the moment.

36. Who is the man _____ that photograph?

37. What time do you expect to arrive _______ the hotel?

38. ______ the Middle Ages people died very young.

39. Ann and I arrived ________ the same time.

40. When I'm bored _______ the afternoon I usually call a friend.

Passive

Passiv

Bildung

Subjekt + Form von to be + 3. Form des Verbs

Verwendung

Du verwendest das Passiv, wenn es nicht wichtig oder ohnehin klar ist, wer eine Handlung ausführt oder ausgeführt hat, und du die Handlung hervorheben willst.

Möchtest du zusätzlich erwähnen, wer die Handlung ausgeführt hat, dann geht das so:

Subjekt + Form von to be + 3. Form des Verbs + by + Objekt

Solltest du einen aktiven Satz ins Passiv setzen müssen, so musst du den/die Handelnde/n nicht erwähnen (= kein "by + Objekt"), wenn das Subjekt des aktiven Satzes "somebody, nobody, people, they ..." heißt, wenn also der/die Handelnde nicht näher bestimmt ist.

Ü 17

Ergänze die Passivformen in der entsprechenden Zeit:

1. All the Harry Potter books ____________________ (translate) into German. (present perfect tense)
2. When Mr Stevenson tried to stop the thief he ____________________ (knock) down by the criminal. (past tense)
3. This dirt road ____________________ (not/use) very often for regular traffic. (present tense)
4. The flight ____________________ (cancel) due to bad weather conditions. (past tense)
5. On your first day at the new school you ____________________ (take) to your classroom. (future tense)

6. In Florida even children ______________________________ (put) into prison. (present tense)

7. If you want to travel to the USA your fingerprints ____________________ (take) at the airport. (future tense)

8. Last year fewer people _______________________ (kill) in road accidents. (past tense)

9. The service at this hotel is excellent. Since our arrival we _________________________ (look after) very well. (present perfect tense)

10. She didn't know if her friend ____________________________ (invite) to the party too. (past perfect tense)

11. Last year the price for gas/petrol _________________________ (raise) several times. (past tense)

12. They told me that everything was okay. I soon realized that I ___________________ ____________ (not/tell) the truth. (past perfect tense)

13. The students ______________________________ (not/give) any homework the week before the holidays. (future tense)

14. ___________________________ (you/examine) by a male or a female doctor? (past tense)

15. A lot of food ________________________ (export) to developing countries. (present tense)

16. A new cinema _________________________ (open) in town. (present perfect tense)

17. A vast area ______________________________ (destroy) by the flood and many people ___________________________ (kill). (past tense)

18. At the job interview you _________________________ (ask) a lot of questions. (future tense)

19. All the injured people ___________________________ (take) to the hospital. (past tense)

20. Large parts of the rainforests ______________________ (cut) down by the countries of Central America. (present perfect tense)

21. Our school _______________________ (clean) every day. (present tense)

22. When I knocked at the door it __________________________ (not/ open) by Mr Audrey but by his daughter. (past tense)

23. The murder ______________________ (investigate) by the CSI (= Crime Scene Investigation) team. (present progressive tense)
24. Aspirin ______________________ (can buy) without a doctor's prescription. (present tense)
25. Somebody smashed the rear window of my car but nothing ______________________ (steal). (past tense)
26. The "Kronen Zeitung" ______________________ (read) by thousands of people every day. (present tense)
27. The famous painting ______________________ (buy) by a Japanese millionaire. (present perfect tense)
28. The police told the bank manager that one of the bank robbers ______________________ (catch). (past perfect tense)
29. Historians believe that America ______________________ (discover) by the Vikings. (past tense)
30. My dad ______________________ (offer) a new job in Brazil. (present perfect tense)
31. Ron and his sister ______________________ (bring) up by their grandparents. (past tense)
32. If you commit a crime you ______________________ (punish). (future tense)
33. They went to the party although they ______________________ (not/invite). (past perfect tense)
34. When ____________ cars ____________ (invent)? (past tense)
35. If it rains the concert ______________________ (postpone). (future tense)
36. The tourists ______________________ (kidnap) by rebels on their way through the desert. (past tense)
37. When we came to the sports stadium we found out that the match ______________________ (cancel). (past perfect tense)
38. Can I use the computer? No, sorry. It ______________________ (use) at the moment. (present progressive tense)
39. A mystery is something that ______________________ (cannot explain). (present tense)
40. The photocopier is working again. It ______________________ (repair). (present perfect tense)

41. If there are any problems they ______________________________ (solve). (future tense)
42. I ______________________________ (often/ask) if it is difficult to be a teacher nowadays. (present perfect tense)
43. My aunt ______________________________ (almost kill) in a car accident. (past tense)
44. Many houses ______________________________ (damage) by the storm. (present perfect tense)
45. Teenagers ______________________________ (often/pay) very little money for the jobs they do. (present tense)

Ü 18

Mache eigene Passivsätze. Verwende die vorgegebenen Zeiten:

1. a new planet/discover/two American scientists (present perfect tense)
2. millions of Jews/kill/in World War II (past tense)
3. a lot of pollution/cause/ heavy traffic (present tense)
4. the victim/kill/with a bread knife (past perfect tense)
5. he/stop/for speeding (past tense)
6. taxes/have to raise/next year (future tense)
7. St. Paul's Cathedral in London /design/Christopher Wren (past tense)
8. the house/surround/beautiful gardens (present tense)
9. the woman/stab/with a penknife (past perfect tense)
10. we/show/the sights of the city/a tour guide (past tense)
11. he/teach/maths/his uncle (present perfect tense)
12. her bedroom wall/cover/with posters of her favourite singer (present tense)
13. the parents of the injured child/inform/the police (present perfect tense)
14. the photos/take/in Cracow/last spring (past tense)
15. most of the earth's surface/cover/water (present tense)
16. Microsoft/found/Bill Gates (past tense)
17. the letter/post/tomorrow morning (future tense)
18. a new hotel/build/near the airport (present perfect tense)
19. Jill/like/everybody (present tense)
20. I/wake up/loud screaming from next door (past tense)
21. the tired child/have to carry/his father (present tense)
22. the fire/extinguish (= löschen)/100 firefighters (past tense)

23. George/attack/a tiger/in the zoo (past perfect tense)
24. the film star/excpect to arrive/any minute (present tense)
25. the dishes/not wash/properly (present perfect tense)
26. the victims of the bomb attack/not forget (future tense)
27. a lot of stones/throw/angry football fans (past tense)
28. the mountain road/close/due to landslides (= Muren) (past perfect tense)
29. my laptop/steal/burglar (past tense)
30. nothing/decide/before next Friday (future tense)
31. some new tombs (= Gräber)/discover/in Egypt (present perfect tense)
32. English/speak/all over the world (present tense)
33. last month/more than 4,000 cars/sell/our company (past tense)
34. our school/redecorate/during the summer holidays (future tense)
35. three terrorists/arrest/in New York (present perfect tense)
36. this schoolbag/leave behind/in a classroom/yesterday (past tense)
37. traffic/ban/from the city centre (future tense)
38. the match/cancel (= absagen)/the club (present perfect tense)
39. this painting/do/the famous painter Picasso (past tense)
40. little food/leave/after the party (past perfect tense)

Ü 19

Forme die aktiven Sätze so um, dass Passivsätze enstehen:

1. Somebody has broken all the windows.
2. People must not leave bicycles in the hall.
3. A lot of people will read this new book.
4. They could hear the music from far away.
5. Someone should have repaired this machine.
6. A loud noise woke me up in the morning.
7. They have changed the date of the test.
8. The government will introduce new taxes.
9. People say that Arthur is very rich.
10. The principal announced the date for the school ball.
11. They have installed a new security system in the bank.
12. On a clear day you can see the hills in the distance.

13. They will take the injured man to the hospital.
14. They are painting our classroom at the moment.
15. Somebody followed me home from the cinema.
16. Monica writes her diary in English.
17. He hasn't cleaned his room for more than a week.
18. The police kicked in the door.
19. The bank changes the code to the safe every month.
20. The kids had not paid for the coffee.

Reported speech

Indirekte Rede

Wenn du etwas erzählst, dann möchtest du manchmal ausdrücken, was jemand gesagt hat. Dafür brauchst du die indirekte Rede oder reported speech.

Abhängig von der Zeit, in der das reporting verb (z. B. say, shout, ask, answer ...) steht, musst du die Zeiten in der reported speech ändern oder nicht.

1. Steht das **reporting verb in present, present perfect oder future**, dann **bleiben die Zeiten unverändert.**

reporting verb in — **present** / **present perfect** / **future** ⟹ **keine Änderung der Zeiten**
(Zeit wie in direkter Rede)

Beispiel: Anna **says**, "They **love** London."
Anna **<u>says</u>** that they **love** London.
reporting verb

Our teacher has often **said**, "You **must not be** late."
Our teacher **<u>has</u>** often **<u>said</u>** that **we must not be** late.
reporting verb

At the end of the match the trainer **will say**, "You **played** very well."
At the end of the match the trainer **<u>will say</u>** that they **played** very well.
reporting verb

2. Steht das **reporting verb in der past tense**, dann **ändern sich in der Folge die Zeiten**.

reporting verb in past tense		**Änderung der Zeiten**
present	→	**past**
past	→	**past perfect**
present perfect	→	**past perfect**
past perfect	→	**past perfect (bleibt unverändert!)**
future	→	**conditional (would + Nennform)**

Beispiele:		
	Yesterday the girl said, "I **hate** boring films."	(present)
	Yesterday the girl **said** that she **hated** boring films.	(past)
	Paul explained, "We **left** at 7 o'clock."	(past)
	Paul **explained** that they **had left** at 7 o'clock.	(past perfect)
	Jack said, "I **have** never **been** to Poland."	(present perfect)
	Jack **said** that he **had** never **been** to Poland.	(past perfect)
	My aunt said, "Years ago I **failed** an exam because I **hadn't studied** hard enough.	(past/past perfect)
	My aunt said that years ago she **had failed** an exam because she **hadn't studied** hard enough.	(past perfect/past perfect)
	Mother promised, "**We'll have** a picnic on Sunday."	(future)
	Mother **promised** that we **would have** a picnic on Sunday.	(conditional)

Manche Verben brauchst du normalerweise nicht zu verändern:

- **would**

  James said, "I **would like** to see that new film."
  James said that he **would like** to see that new film.

- **should**

  The doctor told my dad, "You **should stop** smoking."
  The doctor told my dad that he **should stop** smoking.

- **could** in der Bedeutung von „könnte“

  Aunt Isabelle said, "We **could take** the train to Salzburg."
  Aunt Isabelle said that they **could take** the train to Salzburg.

- **must not**

  The teacher said, "You **mustn't cheat** in the exam."
  The teacher said that we **mustn't cheat** in the exam.

Wenn du reported speech verwendest, um etwas zu erzählen, das immer so ist, dann brauchst du die Zeit ebenfalls nicht zu verändern, du kannst es aber tun.

Peter said, "Paris is the capital of France."
Peter **said** that Paris **is** (or **was**) the capital of France.

Stephen's sister said, "I hate milk."
Stephen's sister **said** that she **hates** (or **hated**) milk.

Ms Woods explained, "Whales **live** in the sea."
Ms Woods **explained** that whales **live** (or **lived**) in the sea.

Damit nicht der Eindruck entsteht, dass du die reported speech nicht kannst, ist es aber vielleicht besser, auch in diesen Fällen die Zeit zu verändern.

Im gesprochenen Englisch werden die Zeiten oft nicht verändert.

"Paul is in the cinema."	Samuel said that Paul is in the cinema.
"We met them on Friday."	Ann said that they met them on Friday.
"Mike will help Simon."	They said that Mike will help Simon.

Es gibt andere Veränderungen, die du vornehmen musst, wenn du Sätze in die indirekte Rede setzt. (Meist nur, wenn das reporting verb in der past tense steht):

now	→	then
here	→	there
this	→	that
these	→	those
today	→	that day
yesterday	→	the day before
last week	→	the week before/the previous week
last month	→	the month before/the previous month
last year	→	the year before/the previous year
tomorrow	→	the next day
next week	→	the following week
next month	→	the following month
next year	→	the following year

Bei der Veränderung der Zeitangaben ist allerdings zu berücksichtigen, **wann** du eine Rede wiedergibst. Erzählst du etwas, was dir jemand gesagt hat, am selben Tag, dann kannst du die ursprünglichen Zeitformen verwenden. Pass aber auf, wenn du Übungssätze in die reported speech setzen musst. Hier ist meist nicht ersichtlich, **wann** gesprochen wurde. Du gehst daher meist sicherer, wenn du die Veränderungen vornimmst, also die Zeiten den Regeln entsprechend änderst.

Ü 20 Setze in die reported speech:

1. Tim complained, "My mother always comes into my room without knocking at the door first. I think this is annoying."
2. Mrs Price said, "I haven't seen the new film with Brad Pitt."
3. Mr Drummond told Mike, "You can use my telephone to call the ambulance."
4. The shopkeeper explained, "I must do all the work myself."
5. The boys complained, "We're waiting for the bus home. It is late as usual."
6. Sue adds, "They'll never tell you what really happened."
7. Peter admitted to his friend, "I told my parents the truth about my grades two weeks ago."
8. Susan said, "We are having a wonderful time at the seaside."
9. The teacher says, "This new book by Stephen King is very interesting."
10. Bob replied, "I've never seen such a cute puppy. I'd like to have a dog too."
11. Mother reminded Alex, "You must load the dishwasher after lunch."
12. Philip explains to Denise, "We may not come to the cinema with you."
13. Tina told us, "Sheila lost her keys last week and never got them back."
14. Anna replied, "I'm sure Simon will pass the exam."
15. The boy insisted, "I gave the teacher my homework last lesson. He must have it."
16. My father explained, "This is the best place for a picnic."
17. The headmaster announced, "I am now going to read the results of the final exams."
18. The waiter promised the lady, "I'll bring your drink right away."
19. The criminal claimed, "I wasn't anywhere near the scene of the murder."
20. He boasted (= prahlen), "Our team will easily beat yours."
21. Jane said, "I wanted to make a phone call to Norway but I didn't know their country code."
22. Richard explained, "I got up late and missed the bus. That is why I am late."
23. Daniel told me, "I am playing in the school basketball team."
24. Dad answered, "We can't renovate the house because we can't afford it."
25. Jack admitted, "I've lost the map and I don't know where we are."
26. Jenny said, "As soon as I have finished this book, I am going to write some e-mails to my friends."
27. The principal announced, "Smoking is not allowed in the school building."

28. Carol promised, "I won't open the door to anybody I don't know."
29. Harry whispered, "I have hurt my arm but I don't think it is broken."
30. Nina explained, "Some time ago we watched this film about a man who only ate McDonald's food for a month."
31. Eve agreed, "Chinese is a lot more difficult than English."
32. My brother has admitted, "I was scared of the dark when I was five."
33. Malcolm insisted, "I know the answer. I just need more time."
34. The teacher admitted, "I was wrong. You did not download the text from the internet."
35. My mum promised, "You will get a new computer if you pass the exam."
36. Kevin told me, "I want to become a software engineer."
37. Dad said, "Someone stole my mobile phone on the underground."
38. Laura explained, "I hate doing revision exercises. I think they are boring."

Questions in reported speech

1. Entscheidungsfragen

Willst du eine Entscheidungsfrage (= eine Frage, auf die du mit JA oder NEIN antwortest) in die indirekte Rede setzen, so brauchst du als einleitendes Wort "if".

She wanted to know **if** (= ob) I was tired.
We asked our teacher **if** we had to write the essay for the next lesson.
George is on the phone. He wants to know **if** you want to come with him.

2. Fragen mit Fragewort

Wenn du eine Frage, die durch ein **Fragewort** (when, where, why ...) eingeleitet wird, in die reported speech setzt, dann brauchst du **keine Umschreibung mit do/does/did**.

"Where did you put the book?" she asked.	She asked where I had put the book.
"When will you come home?" Sean asked her.	Sean asked her when she would come home.
Brad asks me, "Why are you a vegetarian?"	Brad asks me why I am a vegetarian.

Ü 21

Setze die Fragen in die reported speech:

1. She asked, "Where will Simon be staying?"
2. He wanted to know, "Why did Jack and Sue leave so suddenly?"
3. He asked, "Can I book this room?"
4. The manager asked my dad, "Have you ever been out of work?"
5. Father wanted to know, "Will you have time to help me on Saturday?"
6. Uncle Fred has just asked me, "How many English lessons do you have a week?"
7. The doctor asked Paul, "Do you have to wear glasses?"
8. Tom asked his sister, "Can you help me with my maths exercise?"
9. The police wanted to know, "Where does he work?"
10. Tim asked his mum, "Can I help you in the kitchen?"
11. She wants to know, "Where do they keep their tools?"
12. Mum asked me, "When did you buy that nice blouse?"
13. He wanted to know, "Agnes, have you finished your lunch?"
14. Dad asked me, "What is Michael doing at the moment?"
15. My friend wanted to know, "When will you be back?"
16. The man asks the shop assistant, "Do you know any good books about computers?"
17. My father asked me, "Did you remember to feed the dog?"
18. Elizabeth wanted to know, "Michael, why have you turned off the TV?"
19. Tony wondered, "Why is Suzie always late?"
20. Nick asked us, "Have you ever been to Hungary?"
21. Nelly wanted to know, "Iris, do you forget your books on purpose (= absichtlich)?"
22. Tim asked, "How was the party at the weekend?"
23. Max wanted to know, "Bernd, who do you sit next to in class?"
24. Elvira asked him, "Why are you in such a bad mood?"
25. Mum wants to know, "Did you have a good time at the mall?"
26. The teacher asked Becky, "What are your plans for the future?"
27. The child wanted to know, "How tall will I be when I am grown up?"
28. Gregory wondered, "When was the film made?"
29. The tourist asked, "Where is the nearest post-office?"
30. The police asked the witness, "Did you see who caused the accident?"
31. We were asked, "How long are you going to stay in France?"

32. The man wanted to know, "Can I call you back?"
33. Larissa asked her teacher, "How was my English test?"
34. Mum wanted to know, "Do you want something for your headache?"
35. The woman asked, "How much are the shopping bags?"

Infinitive in reported speech

Befehle/Bitten/Anweisungen in der indirekten Rede

Wenn du eine Anweisung, eine Bitte oder einen Befehl in der reported speech wiedergeben willst, dann kannst du das mit Hilfe des Infinitivs tun.

reporting verb + Objekt + to + Infinitiv

oder

reporting verb + Objekt + NOT + to + Infinitiv

"Close the door, please", Mrs Black said.
Mrs Black asked me to close the door.

reporting verb (asked) — *Objekt* (me) — *to + Infinitiv* (to close)

The policeman said, "Don't touch anything in the room!"
The policeman ordered them not to touch anything in the room.

reporting verb (ordered) — *Objekt* (them) — *not + to + Infinitiv* (not to touch)

"Give Sarah the pencil," the teacher said to Mark.
The teacher told Mark to give Sarah the pencil.

reporting verb (told) — *Objekt* (Mark) — *to + Infinitiv* (to give)

Je nachdem, ob es sich um eine Bitte, eine Aufforderung oder einen Befehl handelt, solltest du als reporting verb **"ask"** (Bitte), **"tell"** (Aufforderung) oder **"order"** (Befehl) verwenden.

Ü 22 Setze die Bitten, Aufforderungen oder Befehle in die reported speech:

1. The teacher told the pupil, "Take the letter to the headmaster."
2. Mr Brown warned the stranger, "Leave my wife alone!"
3. Mum shouted, "Don't eat any sweets before dinner!"
4. The teacher admonished (= ermahnen) the students, "Pay attention or you won't know what to do."
5. The man said to the customer, "Please, have a seat."
6. The policeman told the tourists, "Don't step on the grass."
7. The man warned his son, "Don't download any films from the internet."
8. Tina told her brother, "Get off my bed."
9. The woman said to her husband, "Stop complaining about the weather."
10. The crime scene investigator told them, "Don't touch anything."
11. The general told his soldiers, "Attack the enemy!"
12. The teacher asked the shy girl, "Please speak up!"
13. She said to us, "Go to bed before midnight."
14. Dad asked mum, "Please help me look for my reading glasses."
15. The man begged the police, "Catch the thief! Don't let him escape!"
16. He told them, "Stop that noise immediately."
17. The teacher said to the pupil, "Please blow your nose."
18. The principal said to the secretary, "Don't come into my office without knocking first."
19. The trainer told the kids, "Don't leave any money lying around."
20. Mum told Elvis, "Don't kick your brother."
21. My aunt asked me, "Please, pass me the sugar."
22. The man asked the waiter, "Please, bring me a new glass."
23. Dad told his son, "Don't spend all your pocket money on stupid magazines."
24. The life guard told the swimmers, "Get out of the water quickly."
25. The lady at the reception desk asked the woman, "Please tell me your name."
26. The little boy asked his mother, "Please, let me have another cookie."
27. The parents told their kids, "Be careful on the way home from the disco."
28. The girl asked her friend, "Tell me what to do about Frank."
29. The teacher told them, "Keep your eyes open."
30. Mum warned Dad , "Don't fall asleep during the play."

Ü 23

Setze in die reported speech:

1. Mark shouted at us, "Turn the volume down!"
2. Zoe said to her sister, "You have taken my new scarf!"
3. Liz said to the boy, "Don't jump into the puddle!"
4. Melanie asked Bob, "Why weren't you at school today?"
5. The boy whispered, "I broke the window when I threw my pencilcase at Tim."
6. The old man told the driver, "Go down the road and then take the first right."
7. Brenda asked her mum, "Can you give me a lift to school?"
8. The waiter warned us, "Don't try the pasta."
9. She wanted to know, "Who built this castle?"
10. Albert added, "I haven't seen Bridget for ages. I don't know what she is doing."
11. Belinda said, "I hope I will be able to take part in the next Olympic games."
12. The doctor warned Charlotte, "Don't try to become as thin as those models in the fashion magazines. That's unhealthy."
13. He wanted to know, "Are the summers hot in New Zealand?"
14. They asked me, "Do you prefer coffee or tea?"
15. Our teacher said, "It is important to know how to use phrasal verbs in English."
16. Mum warned us, "Don't play football in the garden."
17. Charles complains, "There is never any pizza left for me."
18. Mira asked Herbert, "Do you know who wrote the book 'The Da Vinci Code'?"
19. Granny replied, "This trip to Graz is the perfect present. It is exactly what I have wanted to do for a long time."
20. Dad asked us, "Do you think we should buy a bigger house? If we do, we will not be able to afford a holiday for a few years."
21. Conny complained, "Patricia spends hours in the bathroom in the morning. That's why I am always late."
22. My mum asked me, "What's the matter? You look sad."
23. The doctor assured me, "There is nothing wrong with your eyes. You just need new glasses."
24. Donald's parents said, "If you want to find a good job, you will have to study harder."
25. John confessed, "I hid in the toilet because I wanted to smoke a cigarette."
26. The shop assistant asked me, "What size are you?"

27. Her mum reminded her, "Don't accept anything from strangers!"
28. The headmaster informed the pupils, "There will be no school ball this year."
29. He promises, "I will be home before midnight."
30. Tanya told her brother, "If you keep taking my CDs without asking I will tell mum."
31. Larry said to them, "I hope you are all having a good time."
32. Oliver told his friend, "I hate wearing formal clothes. I prefer jeans and T-shirts."
33. Sally said, "We should go to bed. It is already late and we have to get up early tomorrow."
34. Jack's dad told them, "If you want more snacks, go to the kitchen. There are more than enough."
35. The foreigner asked, "Where can I stay for the night?"
36. Steve asked his friend, "How many kids in your class are going to change school?"
37. His girlfriend told him, "I don't want to hurt you but I don't think you are the right boy for me."
38. My aunt wanted to know, "How long have they known each other?"
39. The new pupil says, "I don't know where the headmaster's office is."
40. Marie admitted, "I am afraid I won't pass the exam."
41. The policeman warned the robber, "If you don't put down the gun, I will shoot you."
42. Mum whispers to Dad, "Tomorrow we will know for sure if I am pregnant again."
43. Fiona agreed, "Some parents seem to have forgotten what it is like to be a teenager."
44. Nick explained to his teacher, "I couldn't finish my project because we had a power failure (= Stromausfall)."
45. She wanted to know, "When will the parcel arrive?"

Ü 24

Setze die folgende Sätze in die direkte Rede:

1. She said that she had had enough excitement for one day. She wanted to go to bed.
2. He explained that Peter often went fishing. He loved fishing.
3. Alice replied that they had left the party at one o'clock in the morning.
4. Nora asked when they would be back.
5. I wanted to know if he had noticed his girlfriend's new haircut.
6. Mum told me not to eat the yoghurt in the fridge. She needed it for dessert.
7. Camilla asked me how many English books I had read.

8. They announced that the plane was delayed.
9. The doctor advised me not to eat any junk food if I wanted to lose weight.
10. Kim asked Martin if he was going to change schools.
11. She informed us that there had been another earthquake in Japan.
12. He said that he loved clever computer games.
13. Sue wanted to know when my birthday was.
14. Christopher insisted that he had not played a trick on anybody.
15. Marion asked me if I had ever tried bungee jumping.
16. The ranger told me not to move or the snake would attack me.
17. Sebastian wanted to know if I believed that there was life on other planets.
18. The news channel reported that the ozone hole over Australia had grown.
19. The nutritionist agreed that more and more people were deciding to become vegetarians.
20. Marlene asked how long it took to fly to London.
21. Bianca told her brother to leave her alone.
22. Dean wanted to know if he was allowed to use a dictionary.
23. Cindy admitted that she had not read the text about Australian National Parks.
24. The tour guide warned us not to go into the bush alone. It was too dangerous.
25. She asked her teacher what 'accidentally' meant in German.

Modals

may/might/could/should/must + have + 3. Form des Verbs (= past participle)

Wenn du ausdrücken möchtest, was in einer bestimmten Situation möglicherweise geschehen ist bzw. geschehen hätte können, dann verwendest du folgende Konstruktion:

He **may** / **might** / **could** have put the keys under the doormat. Let's find out.

Sarah **may/might/could have left**, I'm not sure.

Wenn du sagen willst, was in einer bestimmten Situation geschehen sein muss, dann verwendest du folgende Konstruktion:

Carol **must have missed** the plane, otherweise (sonst) she would be here by now.

Wenn du sagen willst, was jemand in einer bestimmten Situation hätte tun sollen, dann verwendest du folgende Konstruktion:

You **should have worked** harder.
You **should not have talked** about the meeting.

Ü 25

Setze die passenden Formen ein:

1. Does your brother drive a blue car? I'm not sure but I ______________________ (might/see) him in town yesterday.
2. I don't know where my glasses are. I ______________________ (must/leave) them at home.
3. Well, wasn't I right? You ______________________ (should/study) harder for the exam.
4. Sorry, I can't find Mr Anderson anywhere. He ______________________ (must/leave) early today.
5. Don't buy this DVD for Nick. Susan ______________________ (may/give) it to him for his birthday.
6. No wonder you are feeling sick! You ______________________ (should/not/eat) so much.

7. Sam ______________________ (must/call) while I was out.
8. Your husband ______________________ (might/leave) a message for you at the reception.
9. You ______________________ (could/pass) the exam easily.
10. I don't know whether they still live in Vienna. They ______________________ (might/sell) their house there.
11. Why is Ann so angry? Someone ______________________ (must/tell) her about Peter's behaviour (= Verhalten).
12. You ______________________ (should/buy) the other table. It was much cheaper.
13. I'm not sure, but Peter ______________________ (may/e-mail) them the text.
14. What's the matter with your cat? The neighbour's kids ______________________ (must/throw) stones at her.
15. So Charles did not meet you at the airport? I'm sure he was there. You ______________________ (must/miss) him.
16. I don't know where my boss put the file. She ______________________ (might/leave) it on her desk.
17. Sam ______________________ (should/tell) his wife the whole story.
18. I can't understand why Eric doesn't call. Well, he ______________________ (could/lose) your telephone number.
19. You ______________________ (should/not/forget) to write to your uncle.
20. The murderer ______________________ (may/throw) away the weapon after the deed.

Relative clauses

Relativsätze geben zusätzliche Information über ein Nomen im Hauptsatz. Ein Relativsatz wird durch ein **Relativpronomen**, also **who, which, that, whom, whose** eingeleitet.

Für **Personen** verwenden wir **who** oder **that**.

The woman **who/that lives in the big old house** is Mrs Anderson.

Folgt das Relativpronomen auf einen Beistrich, kannst du nur „who“ verwenden.

Im **Genitiv**, wenn du also ein Besitzverhältnis ausdrücken willst, leitest du den Relativsatz mit **whose** ein.

The girl **whose book I borrowed yesterday** wanted me to give it back soon.

In Verbindung mit Präpositionen verwendet man manchmal auch **whom.**

This is the lady **to whom** I gave the keys.
I can't see the boy **for whom** I bought a drink.

Das ist allerdings ziemlich förmlich und kommt in der gesprochenen Sprache kaum vor. Man würde eher die folgende Konstruktion verwenden:

This is the lady **who/that** I gave the keys to. *Achtung auf die Satzstellung!*
I can't see the boy **who/that** I bought a drink for.

Vor who/that darf **keine Präposition** stehen!

Für Dinge verwenden wir that oder which.

I really like the book **that/which** my father gave me yesterday.
I would like to have a machine **that/which** could do the homework for me.
Here is the DVD **that/which** you asked me for.

Folgt das Relativpronomen auf einen Beistrich, kannst du nur „which“ verwenden.

That verwendet man häufiger als **which**. Manchmal musst du sogar **that** verwenden, z. B. in den folgenden Fällen:

- Nach Superlativen (the best, the most interesting, the last ...)
- Nach: all, everything/-body, anything/-body, something/-body, the only, nothing, nobody ...

This is the **best** thing **that** can happen to us!
Let's think of **something that** could be interesting for all of us!

Das Relativpronomen (who, which, that) auslassen?

- Du musst **who**, **which** oder **that** verwenden, wenn es das Subjekt des Relativsatzes ist.

The man **who/that** lives in the yellow house is a painter.
The man lives in the yellow house.

Can I see the book **which/that** was on the table?
The book was on the table.

In beiden Fällen ist **who/that** (= the man/the book) das Subjekt des Relativsatzes und darf nicht ausgelassen werden.

- Wenn **who**, **which** oder **that** das Objekt des Relativsatzes ist, dann kannst du es auslassen. Das erkennst du daran, dass nach dem Relativpronomen ein Nomen oder Pronomen steht.

This is the sweater **that/which** I bought for my mum's birthday.
I bought **a sweater** for my mum's birthday.

You should call the boy **who/that** you met yesterday.
You met **a boy** yesterday.

In beiden Fällen ist **who**, **which** oder **that** das Objekt des Relativsatzes, und du kannst es daher auslassen.

This is the sweater I bought for my mum's birthday.
You should call the boy you met yesterday.

Ü 26

Ergänze who, which, that oder whose:

1. An old woman, ____________ was carrying a shopping bag, knocked at the door.
2. The museum, ____________ was in a historic building, was closed.
3. The couple ____________ house we bought both worked as teachers.
4. The girl ____________ ruler I had borrowed asked me to give it back.
5. The man ____________ you were talking to is my brother.
6. The food ____________ was left was eaten the following day.
7. The dog, ____________ was lying on the sofa, started barking.
8. The guidebook ____________ we bought explained everything.
9. The room, ____________ was huge, was badly lit.
10. The boy ____________ house I was staying at was a good friend.

11. The policeman _________ we asked told us the way to the hotel.
12. The meal _________ we ate was not very tasty.
13. The teacher _______ usually teaches our class is ill.
14. Tony was the first person _________ I asked for help.
15. Can all the students ________ are leaving put their chairs on the desks?
16. The bus _______ goes to Vienna leaves from here.
17. The woman _________ teaches music at our school also sings in a choir.
18. The girl _______ handbag was stolen went to the police station.
19. The boy ________ party I went to last week phoned me yesterday.
20. Where is the pencil _________ I left on the table?
21. Everyone ______ was there will remember the day at the beach.
22. I know the lady _______ bag this is.
23. The Eiffel Tower, _______ was finished in 1889, is made of iron.
24. The children ________ live next door are my friends.
25. The meal ________ Patrick prepared was delicious.
26. The man ________ wallet I found gave me a reward.
27. Sue read a book ________ she really enjoyed.
28. The friends ________ visited me brought me a present.
29. I wanted to buy the computer _______ was advertised as a special offer.
30. Australia, _____ was discovered by James Cook, is a beautiful continent.

Ü 27 **Ergänze who/which/that, wo es nötig ist:**

1. An old man, __________ was wearing a black suit, got on the bus.
2. Did you see Molly at the weekend? No, Friday after school was the last time ________ I saw her.
3. Do you know the woman _________ bought this new horror book?
4. Yesterday Sue went to this new Indian restaurant. The dish ________ she tried was very spicy.
5. The train _______ leaves from platform two goes to Hamburg.
6. When we were in Australia we got lost once because we took a road ________ ended in the middle of nowhere.

7. Here is a picture of the hotel ________ we stayed at in Rome last year.
8. Have all the students _______ are taking part in the exchange programme with Chicago got valid (= gültig) passports?
9. Is this the CD ________ you ordered by e-mail?
10. I started talking to some boys ________ were waiting at the bus stop.
11. The museum _______ we want to visit is closed on Mondays.
12. I found out that the man _______ I talked to on the plane was a well-known writer.
13. Do you see the man _______ is waving at us? Do you know him?
14. Do you remember the film ________ I told you about? I just bought the DVD.
15. Everyone _______ escaped that terrible flood will remember that day forever.
16. Can you imagine? I almost took the plane _______ crashed last week.
17. The woman _______ won a million Euro in a quiz show was robbed last week.
18. The girl __________ is living across the street is my best friend.
19. Tomorrow we will get back the test ________ we wrote last week.
20. Is this the bus ________ goes to Vienna?
21. Here is a picture of the girl ________ I told you about.
22. Anyone _______ cheats in the test will be punished.
23. I did not like the book _______ we had to read for school.
24. They want to buy a house _______ overlooks the sea.
25. The only thing ______ matters is to tell the truth.

Future

will-future

Die will-future verwendest du,

1. um **Erwartungen und Voraussagen, Hoffnungen, Befürchtungen** für die Zukunft auszudrücken.

   I hope we will be there in time.
   I'm afraid he will not make it.

2. um **offizielle Ankündigungen** zu machen.

   The meeting will be at 7:00.

3. wenn du **im Moment des Sprechens eine Entscheidung** triffst (etwa dann, wenn du im Restaurant etwas bestellst).

   I will have the pizza.

Es gibt einige Wörter, bei denen du für gewöhnlich die will-future verwendest:

hope (erwarten)	I hope Tom will help me.
fear (befürchten)	They fear he will not recover.
expect (erwarten)	I expect there will be lots of people.
promise (versprechen)	I promise I will not leave you.
doubt (bezweifeln)	I doubt she will know the answer.
I'm afraid (befürchten)	I'm afraid they won't get tickets.
think (denken, glauben)	We think they will have a nice holiday.
probably (wahrscheinlich)	I will probably not be at home tomorrow.
maybe (vielleicht)	Maybe he will come at 7 o'clock.

going to-future

Diese Form der Zukunft verwendest du,

- wenn du dich entschieden hast, etwas zu tun.
- wenn du über etwas redest, was du schon geplant hast, oder die Absicht hast, etwas zu tun.
- wenn jetzt schon klar ist, dass etwas sicher geschehen wird.

Look at the clouds! It is going to rain. *(Alles deutet darauf hin, dass es regnen wird. Es ist klar, dass das geschehen wird.)*

I'm not going to drink anything. I'm not thirsty. *(Du hast dich entschieden und hast die Absicht nichts zu trinken.)*

Are you going to buy the CD? *(Hast du die Absicht, die CD zu kaufen?)*

Present progressive mit Zukunftsbedeutung

Wir verwenden diese Form, um die Zukunft auszudrücken, wenn wir etwas, das wir tun werden, bereits arrangiert haben, besonders dann, wenn es um Verabredungen oder gesellschaftliche Ereignisse geht. Fast immer gibt es eine Zeitangabe.

A: Are you doing anything tomorrow?
B: Nothing special. Why?
A: I'm meeting Paul at the pub. Do you want to join us?

Da **going to** und **present progressive** beide für Pläne und gesellschaftliche Verabredungen verwendet werden, kann man oft sowohl die eine als auch die andere Form verwenden.

Ü 28

Setze das Verb in der Klammer in die Zukunft. Verwende will, going to oder das present progressive. Manchmal sind auch mehrere Antworten möglich:

1. Have you heard the news? Harry ________________ (join) the basketball team.
2. Sorry to keep you waiting. I ________________ (not be) long.
3. According to the weather forecast it ________________ (snow) tomorrow.
4. I am sorry I can't meet you in the afternoon. I ________________ (go) shopping with my parents.
5. Careful! You ________________ (knock) that glass off the table.
6. I think our team ________________ (probably win) the match.
7. Mary hopes you ________________ (come) to her party next week.

8. Terry ______________________ (finish) painting his room this evening.
9. My sister __________________ (expect) a baby.
10. Bye for now. Perhaps I __________________ (see) you later.
11. I haven't got any plans for the weekend. What ___________________________ (you/do)?
12. Ann ____________________ (not work) on Friday.
13. Are you free tomorrow night? Sorry, I _________________ (go) to the cinema with Bob.
14. The new school ________________ (open) in September.
15. I'll be late tonight but I ____________ (be) home before midnight.
16. Are you going to be here on Thursday? No, I ___________________ (leave) on Wednesday afternoon.
17. Have you seen the weather forecast on TV? It __________________ (rain) tomorrow.
18. There ________________ (not be) any lessons on Monday.
19. A lot of things ________________ (be) different in the year 2500.
20. I _______________________ (study) engineering next year.
21. Don't carry those heavy books alone! Some of the other children ________________ (help) you.
22. Run! That tree ___________________ (fall) down any moment!
23. I think in the year 2100 people ________________ (live) on the moon too.
24. I have forgotten my keys. What _______________________ (we /do) now?
25. Jean ___________________ (get) her hair cut.
26. If it rains my dad __________________ (take) me to school.
27. I ________________________ (wait) here until Carol gets back.
28. Why don't you come with us? It ____________________ (be) a great trip.
29. I have got no school tomorrow so I _______________ (get) up late.
30. Can you help me? I ______________ (see) what I can do.

Vom Umgang mit Texten

Um eine Sprache zu beherrschen, muss man sie sprechen können. Das übst du in der Schule, wenn du während des Unterrichts etwas mündlich erzählst oder ein Gespräch führen musst. Ebenso wichtig wie das Sprechen sind aber auch das Verstehen und das Schreiben von Texten. Das wollen wir im folgenden Teil dieses Buches trainieren. Zuerst geht es darum, einen Text zu lesen und zu verstehen, später darum, den Inhalt wiederzugeben, und schließlich darum, eigenständige Texte zu schreiben.

Ü 29

Hiking in Yosemite

Lisa wanted to go on a mountain climbing trip in Yosemite National Park. The park lies in the Sierra Nevada. It's two hundred miles east of San Francisco.

Lisa and her friend Kim left for the park on a Saturday morning. After hiking for a few hours, they came to a large meadow. To their left they could see a beautiful waterfall. They decided to set up camp there. Kim took some photos because the scenery was breathtaking.
Lisa and Kim put up their tents. After their evening meal they watched a great sunset.
In the morning, Kim took a photo of a rainbow near the waterfall. She also took pictures of two deer grazing in the distance.
After breakfast they packed their backpacks and started on their hike again.
As they moved through the silent forests, the slopes became steeper, and it became colder too. The mountain air was as cold as ice.
Finally they put on the snowshoes they had brought for the final part of their journey.
The broad tracks of their snowshoes were the only marks on the white snow.
By early afternoon the top of the mountain was in sight. Then the wind suddenly picked up. The last few steps seemed more than their muscles could bear.
At last they reached the top of the mountain. Together they looked down at the valley.
It was a magnificent sight. Kim wanted to stay for a while but Lisa thought they should start back before the snow could cover all their tracks.
Before they reached their camp again, they looked once more at the snow-covered mountain. They had made it to the top of the mountain.

Answer the following questions:

1. Where is Yosemite National Park?
2. Why did Lisa and Kim go to Yosemite National Park?
3. What did Kim and Lisa see near the meadow?
4. Why did Kim take photos?
5. What did Kim take photos of?
6. Why could they not stay long at the top of the mountain?

Ü 30

Floating on air

The Montgolfier brothers invented the hot-air balloon in 1783. They probably never guessed how high or how far one of these balloons could go. When they demonstrated their first balloon they used a huge bag made of paper and fabric. They held its open end over a fire. The bag filled with smoke and hot air. Then it rose into the air and floated for a mile and a half.
Nobody rode in these first balloons. The balloons did not even have baskets for passengers. But airplanes had not been invented yet and people were eager (= begierig) to fly. Hot-air balloons offered the first real opportunity for air travel.
Since then, balloons have become much safer. Their baskets not only hold passengers but also special instruments to help control the flight. Ballooning has become a hobby for some people, for others it is an exciting adventure.

Jetta Schantz took her first balloon ride as a birthday present. Later, she set ballooning records. She set a new women's record by staying in the air for 15 hours and 11 minutes. She also took a balloon 32,657 feet into the air. At that height, the air temperature drops to –40°F. The icy air froze her flight instruments.
As Schantz rose higher and higher, the amount of oxygen in the air dropped. As a balloon's burners need oxygen to stay lighted, the lack of oxygen put out her burners. Then the air inside the balloon quickly cooled. The balloon fell, out of control, to 18,000 feet. At that point, Schantz was able to relight the burners and land safely.

Versuche dir fünf bis sechs sinnvolle Fragen zum Text zu überlegen.

Beispiel: Why could Schantz relight the burners after the balloon had dropped to 18,000 feet?

Ü 31

Working hard to become a star athlete

"Mum, I'm going to watch Miriam work out this afternoon," Tim told his mother. "She has promised to introduce me to Mr Hamilton, her coach."
"Miriam, do you really think you should be working out today? Are you sure your ankle is okay again?" asked Mrs Winters, Miriam's and Tim's mother.
"I'm fine, mum," Miriam said. "Besides, I can't afford to miss practice today. The competition in New York is only a few weeks away."
When they left the house Mrs Winters could not help reminding her children to be careful.
They arrived at the gym. Miriam introduced Tim to her coach, then she went to warm up on the balance beam (= Schwebebalken) with the other girls and boys.
"It always amazes me that people can perform such breathtaking movements on that thin beam. It's only four inches wide!" Tim remarked.
"Yes," said Mr Hamilton, "performing on the balance beam is very difficult. That's why I am glad to have found someone as talented as Miriam. She can be on the US Olympic team, but she must be really determined and she must practise a lot."
Miriam slowly raised her legs and did a shoulder stand on the beam. Tim said admiringly, "She makes it look so easy."

"Well, she is very talented. She combines balance and flexibility," Miriam's coach explained. "She is even better when she is on the uneven parallel bars (= Stufenbarren)."
"What about her injured ankle?" Tim asked. "She must be very very careful. She can't simply jump off the beam but must lower herself very gently to the floor."
"Will she do that?" Tim asked uncertainly.
"Of course, she will! She wants to take part in the competition in New York, so she won't do anything foolish, believe me."
"You're right, of course," Tim replied.
"Are you an athlete too?" Mr Hamilton wanted to know.
"Well, I would not say that, but I am on my school's track team (= Laufteam).
I am not as determined as Miriam, though. That's why I'm not a real athlete like Miriam," Tim admitted.
While they were still talking, Miriam bent forward. She kicked one leg up behind her. Then, reaching down, she gripped the balance beam with both hands. Raising her other leg, she pulled herself up into a handstand.
A poster of the Olympic games caught Tim's eye. "You can do it, Miriam," he whispered.

True or false? Tick the correct answer.

1. A gymnast needs good balance.
2. Gymnastics is an easy sport.
3. The balance beam is about three inches wide.
4. Miriam wants to take part in a competition in New York.
5. Tim wants to become a gymnast too.
6. He runs for his school's track team.

Answer the following questions:

7. What kind of sport does Miriam do?
8. Who is Miriam's coach?
9. Why can Miriam not afford to miss a practice session?
10. Why should Miriam not just jump off the beam?
11. Why is Tim fascinated when he watches his sister on the balance beam?
12. Why does Tim not think that he is a real athlete?

Ü 32

Lies dir den Text zuerst genau durch. Dann versuche eine Zusammenfassung (= summary) zu schreiben.

Vergiss nicht, dass ein summary nur die wichtigsten Informationen enthalten soll.

Talking Hands

Alex wanted to write an article on American Sign Language for the school magazine. As he knew very little about sign language and lip reading, he called the principal of the Haymen School for the Deaf (= Gehörlose) and asked for an interview.
When Alex arrived at the school, he was welcomed by Dr Eva Norton, the principal of the Haymen School for the Deaf.

"Sign language is a language of gestures and hand symbols," said Dr Norton. "Many people in the United States who are hearing impaired (= hörgeschädigt) use American Sign Language."
"Is it true that American Sign Language was not accepted as a true language until the 1960s?" Alex asked.
"Yes. Many teachers and parents did not want to use it. Now, though, it's one of the main ways of training hearing impaired people. It makes it possible for them to communicate. Ameslan, a shorter word for American Sign Language, is based on ideas rather than words. The shape of the hand and its position next to the body express certain ideas."
"Dr Norton, somebody told me that about sixty percent of Ameslan is based on the French system," Alex remarked.
"That's true," she said. "You see, the first teacher of hearing impaired people came from France. Laurent Clerc, a deaf person, taught French Sign Language in Paris. He came to the United States in the early 1800s. Naturally, he brought his sign language with him. Now Alex, would you like to see some of our students?"
"Yes, sure," Alex replied.
When Alex and Dr Norton entered a classroom, they were greeted by the sounds of a popular song. Singing the words, the students clapped their hands and danced.
"How can they do that?" Alex wanted to know.
"They can feel the vibrations through their feet," Dr Norton explained.
When the song ended, Alex applauded. Then some of the students came over to Alex. Several raised their right hands to their temples (= Schläfen). They were signing the word "hello".
"Why don't you introduce yourself?" Dr Norton suggested.
Alex imitated the students' gesture. He faced the students and said, "My name is Alex."
When the students answered, their fingers moved quickly. "They are fingerspelling (= mit den Fingern buchstabieren) their names for you," Dr Norton explained.
When it was time for Alex to leave, Dr Norton said, "Why don't I show you how to thank them? Put your hand on your mouth. Keep your elbow against your body and swing your forearm downward."
The students smiled and thanked Alex too. Then they moved their hands up and down to sign the word goodbye.

Die unten stehenden Satzanfänge werden dir beim Schreiben deiner Zusammenfassung helfen. Du kannst natürlich weitere Sätze ergänzen.

Alex went to the Haymen School for the Deaf because ...
Dr Norton explained that ...
American Sign Language was not ... but now it ...
The first teacher of ...
He came ...
He brought ...
The students can sing and dance ...
Alex learned to ...
The students ...

Ü 33

Lies dir das Interview gut durch. Dann fasse die wichtigsten Informationen kurz zusammen.

Challenge under water

Matthew is a journalist who is very interested in diving. During a trip to the west coast of Florida he got the chance to interview Juanita Ramirez, a deep-sea diver. She earns her living by gathering sponges (= Schwämme) from the floor of the Gulf of Mexico.

Matthew: Your job sounds interesting but also a bit dangerous.

Juanita: Well, it is sometimes a bit dangerous but I love my job. I am only one out of many divers who have different kinds of underwater jobs.

Matthew: Do divers have to study marine life?

Juanita: Many divers are marine biologists, and they do study marine life. But a number of divers do other kinds of important and necessary jobs. Some divers do repair work. They repair holes in ships, or the foundations of dams, bridges, and docks.

Matthew: Wow! I did not know that. What other jobs do divers have?

Juanita: Well, some bring up valuable cargo (= Ladung) from sunken ships, for example gold or diamonds. Once, divers even brought up a load of wheat (= Weizen).

Matthew: Your diving outfit looks quite heavy.

Juanita: It is indeed heavy and very expensive. A good diving suit costs a lot of money because it should also protect the diver.

Matthew: How does it protect you?

Juanita: The suit is made of a thin layer of rubber between layers of heavy cloth. A flat piece of metal protects the diver's chest. Under the suit, the diver often wears several pairs of long underwear to keep warm because it can be quite cold underwater.

Matthew: Your shoes look heavy too. Are they?

Juanita: They weigh about 20 pounds each. They make it easier for me to stand up when I am in the water. And the heavy belt helps me to stay on the bottom of the ocean.

Matthew: Your job and other divers' jobs sound really exciting. Thanks for talking to me.

Juanita: You're welcome. Enjoy the rest of your stay in Florida!

Die folgenden Satzanfänge sollen dir bei deiner Zusammenfassung (summary) helfen:

Juanita is …
Many divers are …
Some divers do …
They also …
The diving outfit … because …
A diving suit is made …
The heavy shoes …

Ü 34

Lies den folgenden Text aufmerksam durch. Dann versuche ihn mit den Wörtern aus der Box zu vervollständigen. Überlege dir gut, welche Wörter in welchen Lücken einen Sinn ergeben.

aware, campsite, depend on, endangered (gefährdet), enjoy, enthusiastically, environment, exactly, extinction (Aussterben), face, habitats, hesitated (zögerte), joined, license (Genehmigung), member, national, organisation, place, protected, replied, respect, save, scenery (Landschaft), thought, uncontrolled, used, watch out, wondering

Animals in danger

On Wednesday Paul's uncle Robert ______________ his sister's family for dinner. After the dessert he said, "Paul, I was __________________ if you'd like to go camping in the mountains with me this weekend."

Paul _____________ for a second. Then he asked, "What exactly do you mean by 'camping in the mountains'?"

"Well, you know I am a ____________ of the WWF and they asked me to write an article on endangered animals in my part of the world. That's why I _____________ it would be a great idea if I went up to the mountains. Let's __________ it, it would be hard to write an article about _________________ animals if I stayed in my apartment in the city."

"Do you mean some of our animals are in danger?" asked Melanie, Paul's sister.

"That's ____________ what I mean," said uncle Robert. "We keep cutting down forests and building shopping centers and roads where these animals used to live. People have to become _____________ of the problem."

"I'll go camping with you, uncle Robert," Paul said__________________. "Can my friend Mike come too?"

"That's okay with me," uncle Robert_______________.

On Saturday morning uncle Robert and the boys started out early. The mountain ______________ was breathtaking. After a few hours they found a ______________ they liked. The boys went looking for firewood.

The three campers had a light meal and then sat back to ______________ their beautiful surroundings. "It's hard to believe that animals could be in danger in a _____________ as beautiful as this," Mike said.

"You are right, Mike," uncle Robert remarked. "In the past, ________________ hunting was the main cause of animal ________________. But now, many wild animals in the United States are ________________ by laws. These laws limit hunting and fishing."

"Why are animals in danger now?" Paul asked.

"In some areas the ________________ is being destroyed by pollution. In other cases the land is being ___________for homes, farms, roads, and highways. That leaves less room for animals to live. Their ______________ are being destroyed."

"What can be done to ________ the animals?" Mike wanted to know.

"Part of the land has to be turned into ___________ parks or wildlife shelters. Rangers have to ______________ for people who are hunting out of season or fishing without a ____________. There are always people who don't care about the environment and who have no ___________ for wildlife," uncle Robert explained.

"I didn't know how much animals ______________ us for their survival. I think I would like to join an ________________ that helps to protect endangered animals," Paul said.

Descriptive paragraphs

Kurze, beschreibende Texte

Descriptive paragraphs werden oft verwendet, um eine Person oder einen Ort zu beschreiben. Du wirst wahrscheinlich am häufigsten vor der Aufgabe stehen, eine Person zu beschreiben. Dabei geht es natürlich nicht nur darum, wie eine Person aussieht, sondern es gibt viele Aspekte, die du berücksichtigen kannst, etwa was er/sie beruflich oder in der Freizeit tut, wo er/sie wohnt, welche Eigenschaften er/sie hat usw.

Lies dir das Beispiel einer ganz einfachen Kurzbeschreibung durch und schau dir genau an, welche Elemente eine solche Beschreibung ausmachen.

Beispiel: Ich erzähle über mich selbst

I am fourteen years old, rather tall and I have blue eyes and short black hair. I like wearing casual clothes. I still attend school but I am not a very good student. I don't enjoy having to sit in a room and studying for hours as I am a real outdoor person. During my spare time, I like playing tennis, which I play at least three times a week. In winter I go skiing as often as possible. I also love listening to pop music and I must admit that I spend a lot of money on buying new CDs! I live in a nice house in a pretty town in the west of Austria. I love Italian food and I enjoy hanging out with my friends.

Ü 35 **Beantworte die folgenden Fragen auf einem Stück Papier:**

How old are you?
What do you look like?
What kind of clothes do you wear?
What kind of school do you go to?
What are your favourite hobbies? Why do you like them?
Where do you live?
What else do you like/enjoy?

Ü 36 **Jetzt, da du die Information über dich selbst vorbereitet hast, schreibe einen zusammenhängenden Text über dich selbst.**

Narrative paragraphs

Kurze, erzählende Texte

Kurze erzählende Texte oder Berichte werden oft verwendet, um zu beschreiben, was eine Person über einen bestimmten Zeitraum hinweg tut oder getan hat.

Lies das Beispiel eines solchen Textes und achte darauf, welche Wörter (z. B. first, then …) verwendet werden, um das, was passiert ist, zu verknüpfen.

Beispiel:

Yesterday afternoon I got home from school at 3 o'clock. My mum had prepared lunch, which we ate immediately. After I had loaded the dish washer, I watched TV for about an hour. Then I got ready to go out with some friends. My friends picked me up at 6:00. First we went to see a movie, then we decided to have a meal at Burger King's. We really enjoyed ourselves. We finally left at ten o'clock in the evening.

Ü 37 **Schreibe die folgenden Sätze auf ein Blatt Papier, um einen kurzen Absatz zu schreiben. Verwende die korrekten Formen der past tense und die korrekten Präpositionen:**

Yesterday evening Jack (get) home (preposition) half past three.
He immediately (make) himself a cup (preposition) coffee and (start) to read a book.
He (finish) the book (preposition) half past five.
Then he (have) dinner. Later he (phone) his friends.
When his friends (arrive) they (go to see) a film.
He (hang out) with his friends (preposition) 10:00.
He (be) in bed (preposition) 11:00.

Ü 38 **Versuche eine Reihe ähnlicher kurzer Absätze über das, was du letztes Wochenende, in deinen letzten Ferien etc. gemacht hast, zu schreiben.**

Wie schreibe ich eine Geschichte?

Hier sollst du einige Tipps bekommen, die dir helfen können, eine englische Geschichte zu erfinden und zu schreiben. Manchmal wird deine Lehrerin/dein Lehrer Reizwörter angeben, an denen du dich orientieren kannst, manchmal sollst du vielleicht den vorgegebenen Anfang einer Geschichte fortsetzen und manchmal wirst du einfach eine Geschichte frei erfinden müssen.

Willst du ein/e tolle Geschichtenerzähler/in werden, dann beachte Folgendes:

- Lies selbst viele Bücher und Erzählungen.
- Versetze dich in die Lage der handelnden Personen.
- Schreibe so, als wolltest du einem Freund/einer Freundin ein Geheimnis erzählen.
- Versuche einen interessanten Anfang für deine Geschichte zu finden.
- Lass den Schluss nicht zu plötzlich kommen.
- Hab Freude am Erzählen!

Schauen wir uns einmal an, wie so eine Geschichte entsteht. Den meisten Menschen macht es ja irgendwie Spaß, Geschichten zu erfinden. Da kann man seiner Fantasie freien Lauf lassen, interessante Leute erfinden und seltsame Dinge geschehen lassen.

- Wie beginne ich?
  Es ist ganz wichtig, gleich zu Beginn das Interesse der Leser zu wecken. Du solltest daher nicht mit einer langen Beschreibung beginnen, in der eigentlich nichts passiert. In den ersten Zeilen muss irgendetwas stehen, das die Leser neugierig macht. Sie müssen wissen wollen, was weiter geschieht.
- Handlung
  Die Handlung deiner Geschichte sollte möglichst fesselnd sein. Schreiben sollte für dich genauso interessant sein wie für die Leser das Lesen. Das, was du schreibst, sollte etwas mit dem richtigen Leben zu tun haben, das heißt, die Personen, die in deiner Geschichte vorkommen, sollten – so wie richtige Menschen auch – auf ihre ganz persönliche Weise handeln und auf bestimmte Situationen reagieren
- Handelnde Personen
  Sie sind das Wichtigste in deiner Geschichte. Wenn deine Personen glaubwürdig und echt sind, werden sie dir sagen, was sie weiter tun wollen. Schau sie dir in der Fantasie an, hör ihnen zu und versuche ihre Gedanken und Gefühle zu erahnen. Je mehr du versuchst, dich in deine Charaktere hineinzuversetzen, desto glaubwürdiger werden sie sein.

- Ort der Handlung
  Der Ort der Handlung ist genauso wichtig wie die handelnden Personen. Wenn sich der Leser die Orte der Handlung gut vorstellen kann, dann wirkt deine Geschichte wahr.
- Wie höre ich auf?
  Deine Geschichte sollte ein glaubwürdiges Ende haben, das einerseits folgerichtig, anderseits überraschend ist. Das ist gar nicht so einfach, aber du solltest es versuchen. Ein gutes Ende muss kein Happy End sein, aber es sollte die Hauptthemen deiner Geschichte zu einer Lösung bringen.

Ü 39

Beende die folgende Geschichte:

"Today's the day" she said. "You knew I'd get you in the end."
There was no use in running any more. No use in hiding. There was nobody here who could help me. She had chased me over to the roughest area, and then, into the woods. There was nobody around for about a mile. I would try telling my parents after I'd come home, covered in cuts and bruises, and maybe then everyone would realize just how bad she actually was.
"They won't do anything," she said.
It was as if she'd read my mind.
"They'll just say what they always do. 'She's a little unbalanced, and you'll have to learn to accept that.' or ,Emily, you know of Violet's background, her parents were alcoholics, and they beat her severly. She lived in a caravan, and now she's with foster parents (Pflegeeltern). Everything has been very difficult for her, and now she has problems in her head.' You know that's what they'll say." And then she laughed. That evil cold laugh, and I knew then she was right. Nobody would do anything because of her mental problems, because of her terrible background.
She ...

Ü 40

Schreibe eine spannende Geschichte, in der die folgenden Wörter in beliebiger Reihenfolge vorkommen:

evening lonely car

to lose mobile phone dark stranger

to steal

weapon (Waffe) friend

to shout to lock

Aufsteigen ... in Deutsch 4

enthält den wesentlichen Stoff der Unterstufe nach dem österreichischen Lehrplan, der für die Berufsausbildung und in weiterführenden Schulen vorausgesetzt wird.

Mit „Aufsteigen“ kann man schon am Anfang des Schuljahres zu üben beginnen oder auch erst später einsteigen, wenn es ums **Überleben** geht. „Aufsteigen“ ist natürlich auch für die Vorbereitung auf die **Wiederholungsprüfung** bestens geeignet.

Pieler, Margit; Schicho, Günter
Aufsteigen in Deutsch – Rechtschreiben 4
So schaffst du die 4. Klasse HS/AHS
(mit Lösungsheft)

Kt., 104 Seiten, Format 21 x 29,7 cm
ISBN 978-3-7074-0756-3

Pieler, Margit; Schicho, Günter
Aufsteigen in Deutsch – Grammatik 4
So schaffst du die 4. Klasse HS/AHS
(mit Lösungsheft)

Kt., 96 Seiten, Format 21 x 29,7 cm
ISBN 978-3-7074-0751-8

Aufsteigen ... in Mathematik 4

enthält den wesentlichen Stoff der Unterstufe nach dem österreichischen Lehrplan, der für die Berufsausbildung und in weiterführenden Schulen vorausgesetzt wird.

Mit „Aufsteigen“ kann man schon am Anfang des Schuljahres zu üben beginnen oder auch erst später einsteigen, wenn es ums **Überleben** geht. „Aufsteigen“ ist natürlich auch für die Vorbereitung auf die **Wiederholungsprüfung** bestens geeignet.

Wagner, Günther
Aufsteigen in Mathematik 4
So schaffst du die 4. Klasse HS/AHS
(mit Lösungsheft)

Kt., 104 Seiten,
Format 21 x 29,7 cm
ISBN 978-3-7074-0768-6

Aufsteigen ...
in ENGLISCH 4

LÖSUNGSHEFT

G&G

1

1. The minister didn't give the journalists **any** detailed information.
2. We found out **some** very interesting facts when we talked to the police officer.
3. I can't tell you **anything** about the meeting.
4. Ms Brown will be with you in a minute. She is **somewhere** in the building.
5. I've never met **anybody/anyone** who spoke Chinese.
6. Would you like **something** to drink?
7. Getting there is not difficult. **Anybody/anyone** can tell you the way.
8. The thieves had stolen everything. There we were without **any** money or credit cards.
9. **Somebody/someone** must tell Joseph to be there on time. Otherwise he will miss the train.
10. Can you tell me **something** about the people who want to buy our firm? Sorry, I don't know **anything**. But Bill might know **something** about them.
11. **Some** people think they can get away with everything.
12. I've no idea where I left my keys. They could be **anywhere**.
13. Sally's grandmother spent everything on travelling. There was hardly **any** money left when she died.
14. Yesterday Sandra bought **some** interesting books in a little bookshop **somewhere** near the church.
15. We didn't see **anybody/anyone** who could tell us **anything** about the history of the castle.
16. **Some** people always see the negative side of things.
17. I can't find **anything** in my room. I think I will have to do **something** about the chaos there.
18. Where are my glasses? I must have left them **somewhere** in the garden.
19. Are there **any** interesting new films I should see?
20. It doesn't matter what T-shirt you buy. **Any** colour will do.
21. You don't have to call a specialist. **Anybody/anyone** can do it.
22. **Something** is bothering her. I just don't know what.
23. Can I borrow **some** of your pencils?
24. I know that you don't want to unload the dishwasher, but **somebody/ someone** has to do it.
25. I'm sorry I haven't been able to find **any** of the books you wanted.
26. There is **something** on TV about the life of gorillas.
27. I can't find our cat Mia, she must be hiding **somewhere** in the cellar.
28. I would like to know **something** about the history of this place.
29. We can show you **some** of our orchids. They are very special. You hardly find **any** of their kind in Europe.
30. Andrew must know **something** about the accident, he was there when it happened.

2

1. Mount Everest is **the highest** mountain in the world.
2. Trains don't go **as fast as/faster than** planes.
3. Last Sunday was one of **the coldest** days of the year.
4. My brother is **the laziest** person I know.
5. I think this film is much **better than** the other one.
6. We were really surprised. The book was **more interesting than** we had expected.

7. Andy and Nick are the same height. Andy is **as tall as** Nick.
8. The last test was difficult but this one is **easier**.
9. This is **the worst** holiday we have ever had.
10. The CD is **less expensive than/not as expensive as** the DVD.
11. London has **more** inhabitants **than** Vienna.
12. These two T-shirts are the same price. The blue one is **as expensive as** the red one.
13. The hummingbird is **the smallest** bird we know.
14. I have worked so hard. Look, my text is even **longer than** Sarah's.
15. I don't understand why I have to be home **as early as/earlier than** my sister.

3

1. Andrew didn't **drink as much as Simon**.
2. Paul is **the slowest**.
3. I can't **do more than this/any more**.
4. Tim has **bought more books than you**.
5. "Harry Potter and the Prisoner of Azkaban" is **not as interesting as this book**.
6. Tim doesn't **learn as much as John**.
7. My brother knows **more people than I do/than me**.
8. Sandra is **the cleverest**.
9. Yesterday the weather was **not as good as today/much worse than today**.
10. Sean is **the most intelligent pupil** in our school.
11. You've bought **more books than we have/than us.**
12. Ann doesn't talk **as fast as Phil**.
13. Could you drive **more slowly, please**?
14. Bungee jumping is **more exciting than skiing**.
15. The last book I read was **less interesting than/not as interesting as** the book I'm reading now.
16. Everyone else in our class is **shorter than Tina**.
17. They paid just **as much as we did**.
18. Peter is **the best tennis player**.
19. My best friend likes **music more than I do/than me**.
20. The Queen of England is **not as rich as Bill Gates**.

4

1. My MP3-player is **as** good **as** yours. They are both the same.
2. My father's car was **more** expensive **than** my brother's.
3. This is one of the **most** famous buildings in Vienna.
4. Sarah is taller **than** her friend Mary but she is not **as** tall **as** her brother.
5. Everyone ate more **than** Sarah.
6. This is a terrible film. It's one of the **worst** films I know.
7. You are a careless driver. You should drive **more** carefully.
8. It doesn't matter what you buy. This present is **as** expensive **as** that one.
9. Andrew works **as** hard **as** all the other students in his class.
10. I think a holiday in the mountains is **more** relaxing than sightseeing in a big city. But a holiday at the seaside is **the most** relaxing holiday of all.

5

1. Norway is too cold in autumn. I want to go to Italy where it is **warmer**.
2. Yesterday I met the **most handsome** man I have ever seen. It was great!
3. This exercise is much too difficult, let's do an **easier** one.

4. This is the **worst** coffee I have ever tasted. I'll never come to this coffeeshop again.
5. I can't afford these tickets. Let's get **cheaper** ones.
6. Sandra is the **laziest** person I know. She spends most of her time sitting there doing nothing.
7. I don't think this is a good MP3-player. I want a **better** one.
8. I thought I was going to fall asleep. It was really **the most boring** book I know.
9. When Mona passed her final exam, it was the **happiest** day in her life.
10. I really like Mary! She is the **nicest** person I know.

6

1. I was so tired that I **hardly** noticed that Paul was leaving.
2. Mother was very **happy** when she heard that Tina had passed the exam.
3. I think she is an **interesting** person. The stories she tells are so **exciting**.
4. Paul felt **terrible** on the morning after the party. He had had too much to drink.
5. Tony forgot to do his homework again. He is an **extremely** lazy boy.
6. My father worked very **hard** and was given some extra money by his boss.
7. I am surprised that you bought the MP3-player. I think it is **terribly** expensive.
8. It's not a book I would read again, but it's **quite** good.
9. Father was driving too **fast** and was stopped by the police. He got **really** angry because it was the second time that week.
10. My best friend is very **ill** and has to stay in bed for a week.

7

1. Stop that noise or I'll get very **angry**.
2. If the machine does not work, you'll get your money back **automatically**.
3. The noise stopped **unexpectedly**.
4. This is such a **beautiful** place!
5. There is an **extremely** interesting film on TV, do you want to see it?
6. Where is that **nice** man who helped me with the luggage yesterday?
7. You could **easily** pass the exam if you worked **hard**.
8. She touched the baby very **gently** because she didn't want to hurt the little girl.
9. These are **good** seats, I can see the stage very **well**.
10. I don't know Mr Brown very **well** but he seems very **nice**.
11. Why does your coffee always taste so **awful**? I've told you often enough how to make it!
12. Where did you buy this beautiful shirt? It must have been **terribly** expensive.
13. Your little son is such a **polite** boy, he always greets me **in a friendly way**.
14. Don't make so much noise, you know how grandma hates it when you talk so **loud(ly)**.
15. This car is **surprisingly** cheap, what's wrong with it?
16. Why does she always look so **unhappy**?
17. It's **pretty** late, let's go home now.
18. The roads were **terribly** busy yesterday. I **nearly** missed the beginning of the play because I was in a traffic jam.
19. I opened the door **slowly** because I had heard a **strange** noise.
20. What has happened to Tom and Sandra? We **hardly** ever meet them.
21. Susan, you look **terrific**! What a **nice** coat!

22. I really enjoyed yesterday's party. Time passed so **quickly**.
23. Last year there was a **terrible** earthquake. Hundreds of people were **badly** injured.
24. It is **perfectly** alright for you to leave early.
25. My best friend usually feels **nervous** before exams.
26. Do you know Christine? She learns new languages **incredibly quickly**.
27. His house is at the end of Wandsworth Road. You will find it **easily**.
28. You should ask Ann to help you. She speaks English **fluently**.
29. What's the matter with Peter? He is **unusually** quiet.
30. I'm glad Tim looks **fit** again. He was **seriously** ill last year.
31. It was raining **heavily** when we left the theatre.
32. I had an accident last week. Fortunately, the car was only **slightly** damaged.
33. I think this is an **extremely** difficult exercise.
34. There is **hardly** any snow in the mountains this year.
35. I like your new trousers. They look **good** on you.
36. Don't ask me about the food at Paul's party! The soup smelt so **horrible** that I didn't even want to taste it.
37. When the doctor finally arrived everybody was sitting **patiently** in the waiting room.
38. Karen was **terribly** upset when I saw her yesterday. Do you know what happened?
39. Who is that **handsome** guy over there? He can't be Monica's boyfriend. She is such a **boring** person.
40. We stayed in a nice hotel which was **reasonably** cheap.

8

1. By the time the firemen **arrived**, the fire **had already gone** out.
2. When Adam **met** Eve at the party he **thought** that he **had seen** her somewhere before.
3. After he **had bought** the computer he discovered that it **did not have** a DVD writer.
4. I went to the post office to ask about my parcel, but they **said** that it **had still not arrived**.
5. The Vikings **sailed** to North America a thousand years ago.
6. After she **had looked** at the new dress for ages, she **asked** how much it cost.
7. When the Millers **had saved** enough money, they **went** on holiday.
8. When Mike couldn't find his keys, he was sure he **had lost** them.
9. First I **studied** for an hour, then I **went** for a walk.
10. I **arrived** at the train station at 7:50, just before the train **left**.
11. The police suspected that the burglar **got/had got** into the house through the garage.
12. The team **celebrated** after they **had won** the final match.
13. If I **had bought** more milk, we would have had enough for breakfast.
14. They **got** lost because they **had forgotten** to take a map with them.
15. I feel sick. I wish I **had not eaten** so much.
16. When she came home she **noticed** that she **had forgotten** to lock the door. Thank God nobody **had broken** in.
17. Pam told us that she **had won** a trip to London.
18. By the time I got to the phone it **had stopped** ringing.
19. When they came to the airport, they **were informed** that their plane **had been delayed**.

20. When I **was** on holiday last summer I **went** to the beach every day.
21. If I **had known** that you were ill, I would have visited you.
22. They had to build a new house because the tsunami **(had) destroyed** their old one.
23. They could not cross the river because the flood **had washed** away the bridge.
24. We **got** up early because we **had** to be at the airport at 6 o'clock.

9

1. I **would have bought** that dress if it had not been so expensive.
2. If we **had had** some bread, we could have made some sandwiches.
3. If he had had time, he **would have helped** us move into our new house.
4. You would have lost your job if the kids **had misbehaved** on the school trip.
5. If I had met George in the street, I **would not have recognized** him.
6. The photograph would have been better if it **had been taken** during the day.
7. If he **had offered** me the job I would have taken it.
8. I **would have picked** you up at the station if you had called me the day before.
9. The burglar would have broken in, if the alarm system **had not frightened** him away.
10. If they had not spent all their money on expensive trips they **would have been able to buy/could have bought** a bigger house.
11. You would not have passed the exam if Mona **had not studied** with you.
12. If it had not been so late we **would have walked** home after the party.
13. If she **had known** about his problems she would have tried to help him.
14. If you had not pulled me back I **would have fallen** off the cliff.
15. If they had not sent a search-party for the little boy he **would have died** in the snow.
16. We would have crashed into the wall if you **had not stepped** on the brake in time.
17. If she had not won the lottery she **would not have been able to spend/ could not have spent** a year in Australia.
18. If we **had run** a bit faster we would have caught the train.
19. If I had known you were there I **would have looked** for you in the crowd.
20. If you **had left** a message on the answering machine I would have called you back.
21. He **would not have become** sick if he had not eaten so much.
22. If you **had read** the book you would have been able to answer the teacher's questions.
23. If they had told me about the meeting I **would have come**.
24. If he **had booked** a flight in February he could have gone to Florida in June. Now it's too late.
25. If you had listened to me you **would not have got** into trouble.
26. If you **had contacted** me I could have told you about the change in plans.
27. We **would have got** lost if the weather had not changed.
28. If he **had not missed** the train he would have died in the explosion.
29. If we had stayed at the party a little bit longer **we would have met** the famous writer.
30. If the weather **had been** nice we could have gone to the beach.

10

1. If I had known you were in hospital I **would have visited** you.
2. If he **was not** so lazy, he would get better grades.
3. If I **had known** that the plane was delayed, I would have left an hour later.
4. If she practised more, she **would play** the saxophone better.
5. If you read more books in English, your English **would improve**.
6. If they had not told me about the film, I **would have missed** it.
7. I would say she is happy if I **did not know** better.
8. If you **had not lied** to me before, I would have believed your story.
9. If Pamela hurries, she **will not be** late.
10. If Sam **had** a bike, he would ride it to school.
11. If I had listened to the weather forecast, I **would not have gone** out.
12. If Margaret **takes** her medicine regularly, she will get better soon.
13. If you **had not told** me to stay out of the sun, I would have got sunburnt.
14. If you feel dizzy, **stop** taking the pills.
15. Your English **will improve** rapidly if you practise every day.
16. If David **did not live** so close to the school, he would have to get up earlier.
17. If Miriam had written a shopping list, she **would not have forgotten** to buy some milk for breakfast.
18. If you **want** to come to the beach with us, I will ask my dad if it is okay.
19. Everybody in my class passed the final exam. If I **was/were** the teacher, I would be very proud.
20. If I **had turned** right at the post office, I would not have lost my way.
21. If you change your mind, **give** me a call.
22. If you **drop** the glass, it will break.
23. If they **had arrived** earlier, they would have got a better seat.
24. If the author of the Harry Potter books **had not found** a publisher, she would not have become a rich woman.
25. If you **are not** careful and **break** the eggs, there will be a mess in the kitchen.
26. If we were late for class, our teacher **would be** very angry.
27. If you **do not turn** down the volume of the TV, you will wake up the neighbours.
28. If Columbus had not tried to reach India by ship, he **would not have discovered** America.
29. Jack lost his wallet and he never got it back. If I found somebody's wallet, I **would take** it to the police station.
30. When it rains, the children usually **play** inside.
31. If our team **had scored** more goals, we would have won the match.
32. If he had more money, he **would pay** for you too.
33. There is a "No Parking" sign. If you **leave** the car here, the police will give you a parking ticket.
34. If people used bikes instead of cars, there **would not be** so much pollution.
35. The train station is not far away. If you **follow** this path, it will take you to the train station.
36. If I had not left my umbrella at home, I **would not have got** wet.
37. If I ever win the lottery, I **will share** the money with you.
38. If I **was/were** a famous pop star, people would probably recognize me in the street.
39. If you don't have any money, **get** a job.
40. If she **had realized** you were tired, she would not have asked you to go for a walk with her.

11

1. He admitted **stealing** the car.
2. My sister forgot **to buy** milk.
3. The thief refused **to tell** the police where the money was.
4. They suggested **going** to the cinema.
5. He promised **not to forget** the book.
6. They seemed **to be** very nice people.
7. He regrets **not studying** harder when he was at school.
8. Has he decided what **to give** her as a present?
9. Have you ever considered **looking** for a new job?
10. I really miss **seeing** her every day in the morning.
11. Are you sure you can afford **to buy** a new car?
12. Would you mind **passing** the salt?
13. He pretended **not to know** us.
14. We asked him to stop **shouting** but he took no notice.
15. Remind me **to post** the letter on the way home.
16. The key is on the shelf. I remember **leaving** it there.
17. Maria suggested **asking** Fred to help.
18. I really enjoyed **meeting** your parents yesterday.
19. When you go shopping, please, don't forget **to buy** the things on the list I gave you.
20. Anne loves **cooking** but she hates **ironing**.
21. Sheila offered **to look** after the kids while we were out.
22. She promised **to come** earlier and help us.
23. I can't imagine Mr Chips **driving** a sports car.
24. People used **to make** fire by **rubbing** two sticks together.
25. He surprised us all by **going** away without **saying** goodbye.
26. I can't help **sneezing**. I caught a cold yesterday from **sitting** in a draught.
27. I know my hair needs **cutting** but I never have the time **to go** to the hairdresser's.
28. He made me **repeat** the instructions to **make** sure that I understood what to do.
29. When he told me that everybody had made fun of him I couldn't help **feeling** sorry for him.
30. When you see Tom, remember **to give** him my regards, won't you?
31. He tried **to reach** the shelf but he wasn't tall enough.
32. I often see her **walking** towards the school after **getting** off the bus at the corner.
33. He translated the article without **using** a dictionary.
34. She stopped **to comfort** the crying child.
35. The doctor told me to stop **smoking.**
36. She apologized for **borrowing** my car without **asking** my permission and promised never **to do** it again.
37. He keeps **asking** me the time and I keep **telling** him **to buy** himself a watch.
38. It is pleasant **to sit** by the fire at night and **to listen to** the wind **howling** outside.
39. We got tired of **waiting** for the weather **to clear** and decided **to set** out in the rain.
40. He wants **to visit** his friends in Canada this year.
41. I enjoy **taking** it easy on a Sunday afternoon.
42. My teacher wants me **to work** harder.
43. Would you like **to play** table tennis with me?
44. It's no use **telling** him to be punctual. He just doesn't care.
45. Last year we decided **to travel** through Australia.

46. I don't mind **getting** up early in summer.
47. My grandfather remembers **watching** the first quiz show on TV.
48. They tried **to find** their way back to the dirt road, but they were lost in the desert.
49. Don't forget **to give** her the invitation to your birthday party when you see her!
50. Jenny didn't finish **writing** her essay until midnight.
51. You are always cold. I think you need **to buy** a warm coat.
52. Peter enjoys **playing** soccer with his friends.
53. I told Anna not to forget **to lock** the door when she left the house.
54. Kim always likes **going/to go** on holiday to hot countries.
55. You've still got that hiccup. Why don't you try **holding** your breath, or **drinking** a glass of water?
56. Richard has always hated **living** in the country.
57. Dad tried **to start** the car, but nothing happened.
58. She learned **to use** sign language when she was still a toddler.
59. Ann prefers **reading** to **playing** computer games.
60. When the teacher came in some kids ignored him and continued **chatting/ to chat**.
61. She appeared **to be** really sorry for **having** lied to me.
62. Do you happen **to know** the exact time?
63. Rose expects **to win** the women's 100 m race.
64. Could you help me **(to) carry** this into the house? It's extremely heavy.
65. I hope **to see** you at my birthday party.
66. In the end, Cybil chose **to leave** school and **become** an apprentice.
67. Mona couldn't resist **teasing** her brother.
68. Oliver, please go to the headmaster's/ principal's office. He wishes **to see** you.
69. What do you intend **to do** about your bad marks/grades?
70. My aunt can't stand **driving** in big cities. She always gets very nervous.
71. My brother asked me **to lend** him € 10 but I am not sure if I will ever get it back.
72. My dad can't risk **losing** his job. At his age it is very difficult to find a new job.
73. You should practise **reading** aloud.
74. His friends agreed **to meet** him at the shopping mall.
75. When the burglar attempted **to break** into the house the alarm went off.
76. Bob and Celine don't get along very well but they can't really avoid **seeing** each other as they are in the same class.
77. Please remind me **to ask** Alice for that wonderful strawberry cake recipe.
78. My grandma told me that she some-times feels like **doing** something forbidden.
79. Regina detests **flying** but going by plane is still the fastest way of **getting** to London.
80. What I mean **to say** is that if we don't hurry, we will miss the last bus.
81. The 14-year-old boy denied **beating** up his classmate.
82. I should have seen the car **coming** but I was distracted.
83. They prepared **to leave** on the first day of the summer holidays/ vacations.
84. You can't postpone **making** a decision any longer. You have to decide which school you want to go to.
85. Jason dislikes **arguing**. Arguments make him feel uncomfortable.

86. I can ask mum for anything because she can't bear **to see/seeing** me cry.
87. What do you want **to prove** by **breaking** the rules?
88. When **checking** in at the airport make sure you don't lose your passport.
89. They were attacked while **waiting** for the train to Salzburg.
90. **Becoming** successful is a lot of hard work.

12

1. Are you really interested **in buying** that house?
2. They couldn't leave earlier because he insisted **on having** a shower.
3. The police suspected the man **of being** a murderer.
4. I'm really looking forward **to travelling** to France.
5. The man prevented her **from jumping** out of the window.
6. His friend congratulated him **on passing** the exam.
7. Would you like a cigarette? No, thank you, I have given **up smoking**.
8. Peter is interested **in learning** English. He needs it for his job.
9. She has been thinking **of looking** for a new job.
10. Jason is putting on weight. He'll have to give **up eating** snacks.
11. Heavy traffic prevented the bus **from arriving** on time.
12. Conny is looking forward **to spending** three weeks in Florida.
13. We tried to stop her, but she kept **on talking**.
14. I'm afraid I'm very bad **at solving** maths problems.
15. The Johnsons had to put **off moving** to a new flat as Mr Johnson lost his job.
16. He apologized **for being** rude.
17. Last year the young tennis player succeeded **in winning** all the major tournaments.
18. I am tired **of telling** you what to do. Think for yourself.
19. As she was bored **with watching** TV she decided to go for a walk with her dog.
20. He dreams **of becoming** a famous pop star.
21. The man was accused **of murdering** his wife in cold blood.
22. I believe the police are on the wrong track. I don't think Adam is capable **of hurting** anyone.
23. Paul can't get used **to getting** up early. He is late every day.
24. Anna is not very keen **on skiing**. She prefers swimming and riding her bike.
25. Can you forgive me **for lying** to you? It won't happen again.
26. I firmly believe **in packing** my own suitcase. Then I can be relatively sure I have got everything I need for the trip.
27. Mona is invited to a party but as she is very tired she doesn't feel **like going** out tonight.
28. I'd like to know more **about cloning**. I think it is an interesting topic.
29. The teacher told us to go **on reading**.
30. Tom is not very fond **of flying** but he loves going by train.
31. I don't think I could give **up eating** chocolate. I am a chocoholic.
32. Martin dreamed **of winning** the lottery.
33. Are you interested **in doing** sports?
34. I don't think you can put **off studying** any longer. You have a test right after the Christmas holidays.
35. When Tanya got older she insisted **on having** her own room. She did not want to share a room with her brother any longer.

13

1. Yesterday we went to see our friends in Linz. We decided to **set off** early in the morning to have enough time there.
2. I don't know what this word means. I'll have to **look** it **up** in the dictionary.
3. Paul and Sandra died in an accident. Now Paul's parents **are bringing up** the children.
4. I must **look for** my keys, I can't find them.
5. Our new house is almost finished. We want to **move in** in February.
6. Peter is a strange person. I hadn't heard from him for months and then he suddenly **turned up** yesterday evening.
7. The flat was locked. The police had to **break down** the door to get in.
8. Last week I wanted to buy something in the little shop in Parker Road. But when I arrived there I saw that it **had closed down**.
9. When we wanted to fly to the USA we had to **fill in** a lot of forms.
10. We went to the theatre yesterday evening and Jane **looked after** her little brother.
11. There was such chaos at the airport. Our plane **took off** two hours late.
12. Why are you so angry? Don't you **care for** me at all?
13. I wanted to take part in the bicycle race but it was too much for me. I **dropped out** after 30 kilometres.
14. **Hold on** a minute, I'll be with you as soon as possible.
15. I don't want to **hang about** for ages without anything to do.
16. I can't stand the busy city any longer. I **long for** a quiet place somewhere in the country.
17. Mrs Anderson is a very competent person. She **sorted out** the problem in no time.
18. Yesterday was a terrible day. It was raining all morning. Only in the afternoon it finally **cleared up**.
19. I had no problem with Greg on our trip through Africa. We **got along** very well.
20. I hate Sam. He always **shows off** when he is with people he doesn't know well.
21. Could you **hurry up**, please! We don't want to miss our plane.
22. They are going to pull down our block of flats. We will have to **move out** very soon.
23. Jess, couldn't you **put on** something more suitable for your sister's wedding?
24. Could you **turn on** the radio please? I want to listen to the news.
25. You want to talk to Ms Miller? Okay, **hold on**, I'll try to get her for you.

14

1. Would you please fill in this form for me?
2. When did the sweet shop in your street close down?
3. I don't want the kids to hang around all afternoon.
4. Bill dropped out of school when he was 16.
5. We have to check out in the morning.
6. Why does he have to show off when he is with his friends?
7. I think we will have to set off early if we want to reach the summit.
8. The plane took off from Heathrow Airport at 8 in the morning.
9. She was longing for a letter from her lover.
10. If you wait a minute, I will sort it out for you.
11. I will have to look up his number in the phone book.

12. Ann told us to hurry up if we didn't want to miss the beginning of the play.
13. They had to wait for the weather to clear up before they could climb Mount Benson.
14. Don't look around and chat, carry on working.
15. I didn't know what to put on for Sally's graduation ceremony.
16. So this is your new apartment! Are you going to move in this month?
17. We waited for an hour, but when nobody turned up we went home.
18. I am not going to put up with your behaviour any longer.
19. Could you hang on a moment, I'm trying to find the number for you.
20. I really enjoyed our visit to the museum. I could have looked at the pictures for hours.
21. Unfortunately, I couldn't see the end of the film. My father turned the TV off because it was already very late.
22. Could you take care of the children while I am getting our tickets?
23. I was looking for a parking space when I noticed that there was a new shop in Kennington Lane.
24. I don't care for opera.

15

1. Peter begged his sister not to leave him alone in the dark.
2. They wanted me to do my homework in the afternoon.
3. Margaret helps her best friend to redecorate her room.
4. I would like my students to work harder.
5. I would prefer my son not to play with the children next door.
6. Our teacher wants us to listen carefully.
7. I would hate you to lose your job because of me.
8. Mother would love us to move to this town.
9. Carol expected her brother to wait for her in front of the station.
10. Mr Brown wants his children to be home in the evening.
11. Sarah would hate me to talk to her ex-husband.
12. My brother begged me not to tell my parents his secret.
13. Can you help me (to) carry this table over to the window?
14. I would prefer Sam to work from home.
15. My parents would hate me to buy such a flashy car.
16. We want our teachers to treat us in a friendly way.
17. I expect my friends to help me in a difficult situation.
18. They would like us to move out of the flat.
19. Where would you like me to put the flowerpot?
20. Our boss begged us to postpone our holiday.
21. Would you like me to wait for the taxi with you?
22. My best friend wants her husband to look for a better job.
23. Our mother expects us to pass all exams.
24. I would hate us to miss the train.
25. Mum would prefer us to come straight home after the concert.
26. I would hate my boy-friend to smoke in the car.
27. Carol helps the children to find a suitable present for their mother.
28. The teacher wanted us to learn the new words.
29. I would love Paul to spend his holiday with us.
30. Charles begged his father to buy him a new Gameboy.

16

1. Were there many people **at** the concert?
2. Turn left **at** the traffic lights.
3. I usually go out **on** Friday evenings.
4. I´ll see you **in** the morning.
5. They arrived **on** Christmas Day.
6. Will you be here **at/on** the weekend?
7. I usually go home **by** bus.
8. On Sunday I often get up **at** 9 o'clock.
9. Tom's grandmother died **in** 1979 **at** the age of 79.
10. I'm sorry, I can't find the book **at** the moment.
11. In the rush hour it's quicker to go **on/by** foot than **by** car.
12. Mozart was born **in** Salzburg **in** 1756.
13. I'm going out to do some shopping, I'll be back **in** half an hour.
14. I'll phone you **on** Tuesday morning **at** about 10 o'clock, okay?
15. It was quite a short book and easy to read. I read it **in** a day.
16. Do you fancy going to the cinema **on** Friday night?
17. Carol got married **at** 17, which is rather young to get married.
18. Hurry up! We got to go **in** five minutes.
19. I might not be at home **in** the morning. Can you phone me **in** the afternoon instead?
20. There are usually a lot of parties **on** New Year's Eve.
21. She likes to relax **at/on** weekends.
22. **At** Zack's party I saw a lot of good friends.
23. I haven't seen Anne for a few days. I last saw her **on** Tuesday.
24. Don't sit **in** that armchair. It's broken.
25. When we were **in** Italy, we spent a few days **in** Venice.
26. Vienna is situated **on** the river Danube.
27. Robert lives **in** a small village in the mountains. You can only get there **on/by** foot.
28. There's a report of the tennis match **on** page 7 of the newspaper.
29. Sue and David first met **in** Manchester four years ago.
30. When I go to Vienna I usually go **by** bus.
31. I'll be **at** work **at** 5:30.
32. He will talk **to** you **in** a few minutes.
33. Our flat is **on** the second floor **of** the building.
34. In Britain people drive **on** the left side.
35. I'm sorry, I can't find the book **at** the moment.
36. Who is the man **in** that photograph?
37. What time do you expect to arrive **at** the hotel?
38. **In** the Middle Ages people died very young.
39. Ann and I arrived **at** the same time.
40. When I'm bored **in** the afternoon I usually call a friend.

17

1. All the Harry Potter books **have been translated** into German.
2. When Mr Stevenson tried to stop the thief he **was knocked** down by the criminal.
3. This dirt road is **not used** very often for regular traffic.
4. The flight **was cancelled** due to bad weather conditions.
5. On your first day at the new school you **will be taken** to your classroom.
6. In Florida even children **are put** into prison.
7. If you want to travel to the USA your fingerprints **will be taken** at the airport.
8. Last year fewer people **were killed** in road accidents.

9. The service at this hotel is excellent. Since our arrival we **have been looked after** very well.
10. She didn't know if her friend **had been invited** to the party too.
11. Last year the price for gas/petrol **was raised** several times.
12. They told me that everything was okay. I soon realized that I **had not been told** the truth.
13. The students **will not be given** any homework the week before the holidays.
14. **Were you examined** by a male or a female doctor?
15. A lot of food **is exported** to developing countries.
16. A new cinema **has been opened** in town.
17. A vast area **was destroyed** by the flood and many people **were killed**.
18. At the job interview you **will be asked** a lot of questions.
19. All the injured people **were taken** to the hospital.
20. Large parts of the rainforests **have been cut** down by the countries of Central America.
21. Our school **is cleaned** every day.
22. When I knocked at the door it **was not opened** by Mr Audrey but by his daughter.
23. The murder **is being investigated** by the CSI team.
24. Aspirin **can be bought** without a doctor's prescription.
25. Somebody smashed the rear window of my car but nothing **was stolen**.
26. The "Kronen Zeitung" **is read** by thousands of people every day.
27. The famous painting **has been bought** by a Japanese millionaire.
28. The police told the bank manager that one of the bank robbers **had been caught**.
29. Historians believe that America **was discovered** by the Vikings.
30. My dad **has been offered** a new job in Brazil.
31. Ron and his sister **were brought** up by their grandparents.
32. If you commit a crime you **will be punished**.
33. They went to the party although they **had not been invited**.
34. When **were** cars **invented**?
35. If it rains the concert **will be postponed**.
36. The tourists **were kidnapped** by rebels on their way through the desert.
37. When we came to the sports stadium we found out that the match **had been cancelled**.
38. Can I use the computer? No, sorry. It **is being used** at the moment.
39. A mystery is something that **cannot be explained**.
40. The photocopier is working again. It **has been repaired**.
41. If there are any problems they **will be solved**.
42. I **have often been asked** if it is difficult to be a teacher nowadays.
43. My aunt **was almost killed** in a car accident.
44. Many houses **have been damaged** by the storm.
45. Teenagers **are often paid** very little money for the jobs they do.

18

1. A new planet has been discovered by two American scientists.
2. Millions of Jews were killed in World War II.
3. A lot of pollution is caused by heavy traffic.
4. The victim had been killed with a bread knife.

5. He was stopped for speeding.
6. Taxes will have to be raised next year.
7. St Paul's Cathedral in London was designed by Christopher Wren.
8. The house is surrounded by beautiful gardens.
9. The woman had been stabbed with a penknife.
10. We were shown (AE auch showed) the sights of the city by a tour guide.
11. He has been taught maths by his uncle.
12. Her bedroom wall is covered with posters of her favourite singer.
13. The parents of the injured child have been informed by the police.
14. The photos were taken in Cracow last spring.
15. Most of the earth's surface is covered by water.
16. Microsoft was founded by Bill Gates.
17. The letter will be posted tomorrow morning.
18. A new hotel has been built near the airport.
19. Jill is liked by everybody.
20. I was woken up by loud screaming from next door.
21. The tired child has to be carried by his father.
22. The fire was extinguished by 100 firefighters.
23. George had been attacked by a tiger in the zoo.
24. The film star is expected to arrive any minute.
25. The dishes have not been washed properly.
26. The victims of the bomb attack will not be forgotten.
27. A lot of stones were thrown by angry football fans.
28. The mountain road had been closed due to landslides.
29. My laptop was stolen by a burglar.
30. Nothing will be decided before next Friday.
31. Some new tombs have been discovered in Egypt.
32. English is spoken all over the world.
33. Last month more than 4,000 cars were sold by our company.
34. Our school will be redecorated during the summer holidays.
35. Three terrorists have been arrested in New York.
36. This schoolbag was left behind in a classroom yesterday.
37. Traffic will be banned from the city centre.
38. The match has been cancelled by the club.
39. This painting was done by the famous painter Picasso.
40. Little food had been left after the party.

19

1. All the windows have been broken
2. Bicycles must not be left in the hall.
3. This new book will be read by a lot of people.
4. The music could be heard from far away.
5. This machine should have been repaired.
6. I was woken up by a loud noise in the morning.
7. The date of the test has been changed.
8. New taxes will be introduced by the government.
9. Arthur is said to be very rich.
10. The date for the school ball was announced by the principal.
11. A new security system has been installed in the bank.
12. On a clear day the hills in the distance can be seen.

13. The injured man will be taken to the hospital.
14. Our classroom is being painted at the moment.
15. I was followed home from the cinema.
16. Monica's diary is written in English.
17. His room has not been cleaned for more than a week.
18. The door was kicked in by the police.
19. The code to the safe is changed every month (by the bank).
20. The coffee had not been paid for (by the kids).

20

1. Tim complained that his mother always came into his room without knocking at the door first. He thought that was annoying.
2. Mrs Price said that she hadn't seen the new film with Brad Pitt.
3. Mr Drummond told Mike that he could use his telephone to call the ambulance.
4. The shopkeeper explained that he had to do all the work himself.
5. The boys complained that they were waiting for the bus home. It was late as usual.
6. Sue adds that they'll never tell you what really happened.
7. Peter admitted to his friend that he had told his parents the truth about his grades two weeks before.
8. Susan said that they were having a wonderful time at the seaside.
9. The teacher says that this new book by Stephen King is very interesting.
10. Bob replied that he had never seen such a cute puppy. He'd like to have a dog too.
11. Mother reminded Alex that he had to load the dishwasher after lunch.
12. Philip explains to Denise that they may not come to the cinema with her.
13. Tina told us that Sheila had lost her keys the week before and had never got them back.
14. Anna replied that she was sure Simon would pass the exam.
15. The boy insisted that he had given the teacher his homework the lesson before. He had to have it.
16. My father explained that that was the best place for a picnic.
17. The headmaster announced that he was (now) going to read the results of the final exams.
18. The waiter promised the lady that he would bring her drink right away.
19. The criminal claimed that he hadn't been anywhere near the scene of the murder.
20. He boasted that their team would easily beat ours/theirs.
21. Jane said that she had wanted to make a phone call to Norway but she hadn't known their country code.
22. Richard explained that he had got up late and missed the bus. That was why he was late.
23. Daniel told me that he was playing in the school basketball team.
24. Dad answered that they couldn't renovate the house because they couldn't afford it.
25. Jack admitted that he had lost the map and that he didn't know where they were.
26. Jenny said that as soon as she had finished that book, she was going to write some e-mails to her friends.
27. The principal announced that smoking was not allowed in the school building.
28. Carol promised that she wouldn't open the door to anybody she didn't know.

29. Harry whispered that he had hurt his arm but that he didn't think it was broken.
30. Nina explained that some time before they had watched that film about a man who had only eaten McDonald's food for a month.
31. Eve agreed that Chinese was a lot more difficult than English.
32. My brother has admitted that he was scared of the dark when he was five.
33. Malcolm insisted that he knew the answer. He just needed more time.
34. The teacher admitted that he/she had been wrong and that I had not downloaded the text from the internet.
35. My mum promised that I would get a new computer if I passed the exam.
36. Kevin told me that he wanted to become a software engineer.
37. Dad said that someone had stolen his mobile phone on the underground.
38. Laura explained that she hated doing revision exercises. She thought they were boring.

21

1. She asked where Simon would be staying.
2. He wanted to know why Jack and Sue had left so suddenly.
3. He asked if he could book that room.
4. The manager asked my dad if he had ever been out of work.
5. Father wanted to know if I would have time to help him on Saturday.
6. Uncle Fred has just asked me how many English lessons a week I have.
7. The doctor wanted to know if Paul had to wear glasses.
8. Tom asked his sister if she could help him with his maths exercise.
9. The police wanted to know where he worked.
10. Tim asked his mum if he could help her in the kitchen.
11. She wants to know where they keep their tools.
12. Mum asked me when I had bought that nice blouse.
13. He wanted to know if Agnes had finished her lunch.
14. Dad asked me what Michael was doing at the moment.
15. My friend wanted to know when I would be back.
16. The man asks the shop assistant if he/she knew any good books about computers.
17. My father asked me if I had remembered to feed the dog.
18. Elizabeth wanted to know why Michael had turned off the TV.
19. Tony wondered why Suzie was always late.
20. Nick asked us if we had ever been to Hungary.
21. Nelly wanted to know if Iris forgot her books on purpose.
22. Tim asked how the party at the weekend had been.
23. Max wanted to know who Bernd sat next to in class.
24. Elvira asked him why he was in such a bad mood.
25. Mum wants to know if we/I had a good time at the mall.
26. The teacher asked Becky what her plans for the future were.
27. The child wanted to know how tall he/she would be when he/she was grown up.
28. Gregory wondered when the film had been made.
29. The tourist asked where the nearest post-office was.
30. The police asked the witness if he/she had seen who had caused the accident.
31. We were asked how long we were going to stay in France.

32. The man wanted to know if he could call me back.
33. Larissa asked her teacher how her English test had been.
34. Mum wanted to know if I wanted something for my headache.
35. The woman asked how much the shopping bags were.

22

1. The teacher told the pupil to take the letter to the headmaster.
2. Mr Brown warned the stranger to leave his wife alone.
3. Mum told me/us not to eat any sweets before dinner.
4. The teacher told the students to pay attention or they wouldn't know what to do.
5. The man asked the customer to have a seat.
6. The policeman told the tourists not to step on the grass.
7. The man warned his son not to download any films from the internet.
8. Tina told her brother to get off her bed.
9. The woman told her husband to stop complaining about the weather.
10. The crime scene investigator told them not to touch anything.
11. The general told his soldiers to attack the enemy.
12. The teacher asked the shy girl to speak up.
13. She asked us to go to bed before midnight.
14. Dad asked mum to help him look for his reading glasses.
15. The man begged the police to catch the thief and not to let him escape.
16. He told them to stop that noise immediately.
17. The teacher asked the pupil to blow his/her nose.
18. The principal told the secretary not to come into his/her office without knocking first.
19. The trainer told the kids not to leave any money lying around.
20. Mum told Elvis not to kick his brother.
21. My aunt asked me to pass her the sugar.
22. The man asked the waiter to bring him a new glass.
23. Dad told his son not to spend all his pocket money on stupid magazines.
24. The life guard told the swimmers to get out of the water quickly.
25. The lady at the reception desk asked the woman to tell her her name.
26. The little boy asked his mother to let him have another cookie.
27. The parents told their kids to be careful on the way home from the disco.
28. The girl asked her friend to tell her what to do about Frank.
29. The teacher told them to keep their eyes open.
30. Mum warned Dad not to fall asleep during the play.

23

1. Mark ordered us to turn the volume down.
2. Zoe said to her sister that she had taken her new scarf.
3. Liz told the boy not to jump into the puddle.
4. Melanie asked Bob why he hadn't been at school that day.
5. The boy whispered that he had broken the window when he had thrown his pencilcase at Tim.
6. The old man told the driver to go down the road and then take the first right.
7. Brenda asked her mum, if she could give her a lift to school.

8. The waiter warned us not to try the pasta.
9. She wanted to know who had built that castle.
10. Albert added that he hadn't seen Bridget for ages. He didn't know what she was doing.
11. Belinda said that she hoped she would be able to take part in the next Olympic games.
12. The doctor warned Charlotte not to try to become as thin as those models in the fashion magazines. That was unhealthy.
13. He wanted to know if the summers in New Zealand were hot.
14. They asked me if I preferred coffee or tea.
15. Our teacher said that it was important to know how to use phrasal verbs in English.
16. Mum warned us not to play football in the garden.
17. Charles complains that there is never any pizza left for him.
18. Mira asked Herbert if he knew who had written the book 'The Da Vinci Code'.
19. Granny replied that that trip to Graz was the perfect present. It was exactly what she had wanted to do for a long time.
20. Dad asked us if we thought we should buy a bigger house. If we did, we would not be able to afford a holiday for a few years.
21. Conny complained that Patricia spent hours in the bathroom in the morning. That was why she was always late.
22. My mum asked me what the matter was. I looked sad.
23. The doctor assured me that there was nothing wrong with my eyes. I just needed new glasses.
24. Donald's parents said that if he wanted to find a good job, he would have to study harder.
25. John confessed that he had hidden in the toilet because he had wanted to smoke a cigarette.
26. The shop assistant asked me what size I was.
27. Her mum reminded her not to accept anything from strangers.
28. The headmaster informed the pupils that there would be no school ball that year.
29. He promises that he will be home before midnight.
30. Tanya told her brother that if he kept taking her CDs without asking she would tell mum.
31. Larry said to them that he hoped they were all having a good time.
32. Oliver told his friend that he hated wearing formal clothes. He preferred jeans and T-shirts.
33. Sally said that they should go to bed. It was already late and they had to get up early the next day.
34. Jack's dad told them that if they wanted more snacks, they should go to the kitchen. There were more than enough.
35. The foreigner asked where he could stay for the night.
36. Steve asked his friend how many kids in his class were going to change school.
37. His girlfriend told him that she didn't want to hurt him but she didn't think he was the right boy for her.
38. My aunt wanted to know how long they had known each other.
39. The new pupil says that he/she doesn't know where the headmaster's office is.
40. Marie admitted that she was afraid she wouldn't pass the exam.
41. The policeman warned the robber that if he didn't put down the gun, he would shoot him.

42. Mum whispers to Dad that tomorrow they will know for sure if she is pregnant again.
43. Fiona agreed that some parents seemed to have forgotten what it was like to be a teenager.
44. Nick explained to his teacher that he hadn't been able to finish his project because they had had a power failure.
45. She wanted to know when the parcel would arrive.

24

1. She said, "I have had enough excitement for one day. I want to go to bed."
2. He explained, "Peter often goes fishing. He loves fishing."
3. Alice replied, "We left the party at one o'clock in the morning."
4. Nora asked, "When will you be back?"
5. I wanted to know, "Have you noticed/ Did you notice your girlfriend's new haircut?"
6. Mum told me, "Don't eat the yoghurt in the fridge. I need it for dessert."
7. Camilla asked me, "How many English books have you read?"
8. They announced, "The plane is delayed."
9. The doctor advised me, "Don't eat any junk food if you want to lose weight."
10. Kim asked Martin, "Are you going to change schools?"
11. She informed us, "There has been another earthquake in Japan."
12. He said, "I love clever computer games."
13. Sue wanted to know, "When is your birthday?"
14. Christopher insisted, "I have not played/did not play a trick on anybody."
15. Marion asked me, "Have you ever tried bungee jumping?"
16. The ranger told me, "Don't move or the snake will attack you!"
17. Sebastian wanted to know, "Do you believe that there is life on other planets?"
18. The news channel reported, "The ozone hole over Australia has grown."
19. The nutritionist agreed, "More and more people are deciding to become vegetarians."
20. Marlene asked, "How long does it take to fly to London?"
21. Bianca told her brother, "Leave me alone!"
22. Dean wanted to know, "Am I allowed to use a dictionary?"
23. Cindy admitted, "I have not read/did not read the text about Australian National Parks."
24. The tour guide warned us, "Don't go into the bush alone. It is too dangerous."
25. She asked her teacher, "What does 'accidentally' mean in German?"

25

1. I'm not sure but I **might have seen** him in town yesterday,
2. I **must have left** them at home.
3. You **should have studied** harder for the exam.
4. He **must have left** early today.
5. Susan **may have given** it to him for his birthday.
6. You **should not have eaten** so much.
7. Sam **must have called** while I was out.
8. Your husband **might have left** a message for you at the reception.
9. You **could have passed** the exam easily.

10. They **might have sold** their house there.
11. Someone **must have told** her about Peter's behaviour.
12. You **should have bought** the other table. It was much cheaper.
13. I'm not sure, but Peter **may have e-mailed** them the text.
14. The neighbour's kids **must have thrown** stones at her.
15. You **must have missed** him.
16. She **might have left** it on her desk.
17. Sam **should have told** his wife the whole story.
18. Well, he **could have lost** your telephone number.
19. You **should not have forgotten** to write to your uncle.
20. The murderer **may have thrown** away the weapon after the deed.

26

1. An old woman, **who** was carrying a shopping bag, knocked at the door.
2. The museum, **which** was in a historic building, was closed.
3. The couple **whose** house we bought both worked as teachers.
4. The girl **whose** ruler I had borrowed asked me to give it back.
5. The man **who** you were talking to is my brother.
6. The food **that/which** was left was eaten the following day.
7. The dog, **which** was lying on the sofa, started barking.
8. The guidebook **that/which** we bought explained everything.
9. The room, **which** was huge, was badly lit.
10. The boy **whose** house I was staying at was a good friend.
11. The policeman **that/who** we asked told us the way to the hotel.
12. The meal **that/which** we ate was not very tasty.
13. The teacher **who** usually teaches our class is ill.
14. Tony was the first person **that/who** I asked for help.
15. Can all the students **who** are leaving put their chairs on the desks?
16. The bus **that/which** goes to Vienna leaves from here.
17. The woman **who** teaches music at our school also sings in a choir.
18. The girl **whose** handbag was stolen went to the police station.
19. The boy **whose** party I went to last week phoned me yesterday.
20. Where is the pencil **that/which** I left on the table?
21. Everyone **who** was there will remember the day at the beach.
22. I know the lady **whose** bag this is.
23. The Eiffel Tower, **which** was finished in 1889, is made of iron.
24. The children **who** live next door are my friends.
25. The meal **that/which** Patrick prepared was delicious.
26. The man **whose** wallet I found gave me a reward.
27. Sue read a book **that/which** she really enjoyed.
28. The friends **who** visited me brought me a present.
29. I wanted to buy the computer **that/which** was advertised as a special offer.
30. Australia, **which** was discovered by James Cook, is a beautiful continent.

27

1. An old man, **who** was wearing a black suit, got on the bus.
2. Did you see Molly at the weekend? No, Friday after school was the last time **(x)** I saw her.

3. Do you know the women **who** bought this new horror book?
4. Yesterday Sue went to this new Indian restaurant. The dish **(x)** she tried was very spicy.
5. The train **that/which** leaves from platform two goes to Hamburg.
6. When we were in Australia we got lost once because we took a road **that/which** ended in the middle of nowhere.
7. Here is a picture of the hotel **(x)** we stayed at in Rome last year.
8. Have all the students **who** are taking part in the exchange programme with Chicago got valid passports?
9. Is this the CD **(x)** you ordered by e-mail?
10. I started talking to some boys **who** were waiting at the bus stop.
11. The museum **(x)** we want to visit is closed on Mondays.
12. I found out that the man **(x)** I talked to on the plane was a well-known writer.
13. Do you see the man **who** is waving at us? Do you know him?
14. Do you remember the film **(x)** I told you about? I just bought the DVD.
15. Everyone **who** escaped that terrible flood will remember that day forever.
16. Can you imagine? I almost took the plane **that/which** crashed last week.
17. The woman **who** won a million Euro in a quiz show was robbed last week.
18. The girl **who** is living across the street is my best friend.
19. Tomorrow we will get back the test **(x)** we wrote last week.
20. Is this the bus **that/which** goes to Vienna?
21. Here is a picture of the girl **(x)** I told you about.
22. Anyone **who** cheats in the test will be punished.
23. I did not like the book **(x)** we had to read for school.
24. They want to buy a house **that/which** overlooks the sea.
25. The only thing **that** matters is to tell the truth.

28

1. Have you heard the news? Harry **is joining/is going** to join the basketball team.
2. Sorry to keep you waiting. I **won't be** long.
3. According to the weather forecast it is **going to snow** tomorrow.
4. I am sorry I can't meet you in the afternoon. I **am going** shopping with my parents.
5. Careful! You **are going to/will knock** that glass off the table.
6. I think our team **will probably win** the match.
7. Mary hopes you **will come** to her party next week.
8. Terry **is going to finish** painting his room this evening.
9. My sister **is expecting** a baby.
10. Bye for now. Perhaps **I'll see** you later.
11. I haven't got any plans for the weekend. What **are you doing/going to do**?
12. Ann **is not working** on Friday.
13. Are you free tomorrow night? Sorry, I **am going** to the cinema with Bob.
14. The new school **will open/is going to open** in September.
15. I'll be late tonight but I **will be** home before midnight.
16. Are you going to be here on Thursday? No, I **am leaving** on Wednesday afternoon.
17. Have you seen the weather forecast on TV? It **is going to rain** tomorrow.
18. There **won't be** any lessons on Monday.
19. A lot of things **will be** different in the year 2500.

20. I **am going to study** engineering next year.
21. Don't carry those heavy books alone! Some of the other children **will help** you.
22. Run! That tree **is going to fall** down any moment!
23. I think in the year 2100 people **will live** on the moon too.
24. I have forgotten my keys. What **are we going to do** now?
25. Jean **is going to get** her hair cut.
26. If it rains my dad **will take** me to school.
27. I **am going to wait/I will wait** here until Carol gets back.
28. Why don't you come with us? It **will be/is going to be** a great trip.
29. I have got no school tomorrow so I **will get/am going to get** up late.
30. Can you help me? **I'll see** what I can do.

29

1. The park is situated/lies in the Sierra Nevada, about two hundred miles east of San Francisco.
2. They wanted to go hiking and mountain climbing.
3. They saw a beautiful waterfall.
4. She took photos because the scenery was breathtaking.
5. She took a photo of a rainbow and of two grazing deer.
6. There was a strong wind and they were afraid that the snow would cover all their tracks.

30

Die Fragen könnten etwa so aussehen. Hier nur drei Beispiele:

1. When did the Montgolfier brothers invent the hot air balloon?
2. How long was the first flight?
3. How long did Jetta Schantz stay in the air when she set a new women's record?

31

1. A gymnast needs good balance. (T)
2. Gymnastics is an easy sport. (F)
3. The balance beam is about three inches wide. (F)
4. Miriam wants to take part in a competition in New York. (T)
5. Tim wants to become a gymnast too. (F)
6. He runs for his school's track team. (T)
7. She performs on the balance beam and on the uneven parallel bars.
8. His name is Mr Hamilton.
9. She wants to take part in a competition in New York, which is only a few weeks away.
10. She has an injured ankle.
11. She makes performing on the balance beam look easy.
12. He is not as determined as his sister Miriam.

34

On Wednesday Paul's uncle Robert **joined** his sister's family for dinner. After the dessert he said, "Paul, I was **wondering** if you'd like to go camping in the mountains with me this weekend."
Paul **hesitated** for a second. Then he asked, "What exactly do you mean by 'camping in the mountains'?"
"Well, you know I am a **member** of the WWF and they asked me to write an article on endangered animals in my part of the world. That's why I **thought** it would be a great idea if I went up to the mountains. Let's **face** it, it would be hard to write an article about **endangered** animals if I stayed in my apartment in the city."

"Do you mean some of our animals are in danger?" asked Melanie, Paul's sister.
"That's **exactly** what I mean," said uncle Robert. "We keep cutting down forests and building shopping centers and roads where these animals used to live. People have to become **aware** of the problem."
"I'll go camping with you, uncle Robert," Paul said **enthusiastically**. "Can my friend Mike come too?"
"That's okay with me," uncle Robert **replied**.
On Saturday morning uncle Robert and the boys started out early. The mountain **scenery** was breathtaking. After a few hours they found a **campsite** they liked. The boys went looking for firewood.
The three campers had a light meal and then sat back to **enjoy** their beautiful surroundings. "It's hard to believe that animals could be in danger in a **place** as beautiful as this," Mike said.
"You are right, Mike," uncle Robert remarked. "In the past, **uncontrolled** hunting was the main cause of animal **extinction**. But now, many wild animals in the United States are **protected** by laws. These laws limit hunting and fishing."
"Why are animals in danger now?" Paul asked.
"In some areas the **environment** is being destroyed by pollution. In other cases the land is being **used** for homes, farms, roads, and highways. That leaves less room for animals to live. Their **habitats** are being destroyed."
"What can be done to **save** the animals?" Mike wanted to know.
"Part of the land has to be turned into **national** parks or wildlife shelters. Rangers have to **watch out** for people who are hunting out of season or fishing without a **license**. There are always people who don't care about the environment and who have no **respect** for wildlife," uncle Robert explained.
"I didn't know how much animals **depend on** us for their survival. I think I would like to join an **organisation** that helps to protect endangered animals," Paul said.

37

Yesterday evening Jack **got** home **at** half past three.
He immediately **made** himself a cup **of** coffee and **started** to read a book.
He **finished** the book **at** half past five.
Then he **had** dinner. Later he **phoned** his friends.
When his friends **arrived** they **went to see** a film.
He **hung out** with his friends **until** 10:00.
He **was** in bed **at/by** 11:00.